KEEPING
Life
SIMPLE

Edited by Deborah Burns and Pamela Lappies
Text design by Greg Imhoff
Text production by Wanda Harper Joyce
Production assistance by Susan Bernier and Allison Cranmer
Indexed by Northwind Editorial Services

The information in this book is true and complete to the best of our
knowledge. All recommendations are made without guarantee on the
part of the author or Storey Communications, Inc. The author and
publisher disclaim any liability in connection with the use of this
information. For additional information please contact Storey
Communications, Inc., Schoolhouse Road, Pownal, Vermont 05261.

KEEPING

Life

SIMPLE

7 Guiding Principles
500 Tips & Ideas

by KAREN LEVINE

BOK 5015

Table of Contents

Dedication

For my aunt, Ann Levine, who knows
what matters . . . and what doesn't.

Acknowledgments

Thank you: C.L. Fornari, Susan Engel, and Judy
Francis, who deserve bylines here for the many,
many pages of hints they sent my way; Nancy
Knabbe, who passed on odd and wonderful old
remedies and concoctions; Pam Lappies, my good
friend and editor, who kept my life simple by
making promises and keeping them; and my
family—Alan, Noah, and Nathaniel—who complicate my life in so many rich and wonderful ways.

Early on in this book I stress the importance
of learning to say "No" to people who ask for your
help and your time. Everyone who helped me
finish this book is now free to follow that advice!

Introduction

In this chapter . . .

* *Seven Guiding Principles*

I t's 11:30 PM and you're exhausted. It's been one of those overwhelming days. For most of us each day is packed. Shopping for food, for clothing, for stuff and more stuff. Transporting people, animals, stuff and more stuff. Talking to kids, parents, husbands, wives, employees, employers, friends, and relatives about stuff and more stuff. Caring for people, animals, houses, gardens, stuff and more stuff.

This accumulation of activities, responsibilities, and, of course, stuff comprises what most of us think of as The American Dream. But there appears to be less and less of a positive correlation between the realization of The Dream and the sense of satisfaction we feel at the end of each day. Life, for more and more Americans, is feeling very cluttered, and clutter doesn't lead to a sense of satisfaction.

In a recent telephone poll by the Harwood Group of Bethesda, Maryland, 95 percent of the respondents believed that most Americans are materialistic;

and 82 percent agreed that we buy and consume far more than we need. Among that same group, only 15 percent said they would be much more satisfied with their lives if they had nicer things in their homes, whereas 66 percent said they felt their lives would be more satisfying if they had more time to spend with family and friends.

How do people who feel they are doing more/earning more/getting more but enjoying it all less manage to turn things around and focus on building more satisfying lives? How do we sort through all the "stuff" and find the meaning that we long for? How can we simplify and enhance our lives?

This book attempts to answer those questions on two levels. On a pragmatic level, we hope to help you simplify your life by offering tips and hints for accomplishing tasks and chores more efficiently. We all spend more time than we want to dealing with chores, errands, and the like. The tips we offer in this book are aimed at shaving off valuable time from those tasks so that you have more time for the things that offer you the most satisfaction.

On an aesthetic level, much of what we offer in the pages that follow involves things you can do to simplify, and thereby enhance, your life. These hints aim at redefining The American Dream — making it one that offers you real, personal gratification. In the same poll mentioned earlier, the Harwood Group of Bethesda, Maryland, asked people who had downshifted — that is, simplified their lives — how they felt about the changes they had made, and 86 percent of the respondents said they were happy. Those are pretty good odds by any account.

Not all of the tips that you'll encounter in this book are for everyone, and some may, when read together, seem contradictory. That is intentional. After all, one person's trash is another person's treasure. Different people find satisfaction in different ways. This idea might seem obvious, but you'd be surprised by how many people devote their energies to trying to be happy in a prescribed way, rather than to trying to determine what it is that really makes them happy. The key, of course, is to figure out precisely what your idea of heaven is, and to simplify and design your life so that you can get as close to it as possible while you're still on this planet. How do you accomplish that? Begin with our **Seven Guiding Principles** for a simpler life.

Seven Guiding Principles

These principles apply equally to hints that are aimed at making your life more efficient, and to hints that are aimed at helping you downshift and refocus your energies. Post them on your refrigerator door. Doodle them on a scrap of paper in your spare time. Recite them as a mantra when you lie in bed at night. Think of them as our seven commandments. Think of them as the spirit behind the action. Think of them however you like . . . but think of them often!

Principle #1 — Relax your standards.

A friend once told me how she and her family had traditionally celebrated Christmas. "We had the most perfect Christmas," she said. "It was really a Martha-Stewart-eat-your-heart-out Christmas. Our house was perfectly decorated, and we did it all together as a family. Greens, the tree, lights . . . everything was absolute perfection. And I'd have my entire family over for Christmas dinner. Usually we had a five-course sit-down for about twenty. Everyone was dressed up . . . new clothing, new haircuts . . . really picture-perfect. And after dinner our children would put on a little pageant that they'd put together on their own . . . with my help."

Christmas gifts had to meet the highest standards as well. "I never felt that it was enough to just go out and *buy* a gift," my friend said. "It seemed to me that a gift wasn't really special unless I had made it myself, so I'd spend much of the year knitting and sewing and preparing all of these special hand-made gifts for everyone. And before I even got to work on the gifts there were months and months of just thinking about what would best suit everyone."

My friend's Christmas was, indeed, picture-perfect, and for many years it was a source of great pleasure to her. But somewhere along the line her pleasure shifted to exhaustion. By the time she turned forty she began to dread the onset of the holiday season. "By the time I realized how much I dreaded all the work, I felt trapped in it. My kids were feeling too old for the pageant, I had a more demanding job that offered me less time to make gifts, and I saw absolutely no way out!"

The expectation that *her* Christmas had to meet a certain standard had turned into a trap. Where that standard originally came from, my friend wasn't quite sure. She may even have developed the standard on her own, at a time when it offered her a sense of satisfaction. The problem was that when her standard became a burden, the joy was gone ... and with it, the point of the celebration.

If you're still trying to live your life in a way that will please your mom, your dad, your spouse, Santa, or the powers that be, it's time to stop and ask yourself why. Why does the Christmas have to be perfect? Why does the spread have to be on the bed? Why does the family dinner have to represent a balance of the five food groups? Why does the shirt have to be ironed all the way down if only the collar will show?

If you're struggling to meet standards because you find the effort satisfying, then, by all means, struggle on. If the joy hadn't left my friend's Christmas, she would not have needed to examine her standards. But if meeting your standards leaves you with too little energy to enjoy other things, it's time to relax them.

Principle #2 — Free yourself of stereotypical roles.

We'll talk in Chapter 2 about the fact that we all wear different hats at different times of the day. Mother, daughter, chauffeur, cook, domestic, secretary, accountant, nurse, clergy, plumber, and on and on. Some of the roles we play are by choice. Others are by necessity. But sometimes we play roles simply because we think we should ... even if they are roles to which we are not at all suited.

My husband is an avid gardener and a fabulous cook. I love to cook also, but I much prefer doing carpentry to gardening. Our kids have grown up in a home in which Mom is Mrs. Fixit and Dad is the expert on gardens and flower arranging. During my own childhood it was my father who fixed everything and my mother who cut the roses and arranged them in beautiful vases all over our home. It took me a while to feel comfortable with the fact that the roles in the family I created as an adult were very different from the roles of my childhood. What I realized, however, was that I got a great deal of pleasure from being Mrs. Fixit. I was good at it. I enjoyed being good at it. My husband was as delighted to have me take care of things at home as he was to dive into the things that gave him pleasure. And there wasn't a reason in the world for me not to do what I liked or for him not to do what he liked!

Clearly, it makes no sense to expend energy doing things you're neither good at nor enjoy, simply because those are things that men or women are supposed to do. Think about all that needs to be done in a day, and then divide up the tasks based on inclination rather than on stereotypical roles. Lest you think that everyone is already doing this . . . think again!

Principle #3 — Take time to figure out what you find most satisfying.

We often use the analogy of a treadmill to describe how we feel about our lives . . . running, like a hamster, on that wheel; not thinking about the fact that we aren't getting anywhere, but running all the same. What we suggest in this book is that you set aside the time to think about what it is that gives you the most pleasure and satisfaction.

Chapter 2, which involves keeping track of your time, offers an opportunity for this kind of reflection. We all get into ruts, doing things out of habit rather than because we truly want to do them. For years, I'd stay up to watch the eleven o'clock news every night. In the morning I'd be tired. In fact, I'd invariably drift off during the news, not really absorbing a whole lot of what was being said.

Why did I force myself to stay up and watch it? Beats me, but I know that my parents did the same thing. At some point I realized that I preferred the morning newspaper as a source of news, and that bedtime, for me, was much more pleasurable when I listened to jazz and read a good book. Cool.

Principle #4 — Create time for the things you care about.

The purpose of taking the time to think about what it is you care about (Principle #3) is to make time for those things in your life. If you hate cooking and love reading, why spend two hours on meal-making and allot bedtime (when you can barely keep your eyes open) for your beloved books?

My husband realized, not long ago, that regular aerobic exercise really makes him feel good — both physically and emotionally. But somehow, the days would come and go and there was never time for him to get on the Nordic Track. By the time he crawled into bed at night he was just too tired; and even if he made himself get on the machine at 11:00, it would wind him up in a way that interfered with his sleep.

He was pretty miserable, so we sat down and looked at our day. We came up with a schedule that involved his getting up with my older son every morning, who needed to be on the schoolbus at 7:10 AM. He'd drop off my son at the bus stop and come home to get on the exercise machine, while I'd get my younger son up. By the time I was ready to drop off my younger son at the bus stop, my husband would be finished with his exercising and ready to go out with me for a cup of coffee before we began our day's work.

There's nothing very complicated about what we worked out. The important thing, however, is that we took the trouble to do it. Now, by 8:30 every morning my husband has gotten his exercise out of the way and feels energized to begin his day. It's a little thing that requires a little bit of thought and effort, but it makes a big difference.

Principle #5 — Learn to enjoy what's in front of you.

Last summer my family went on a very much deserved vacation ... the first in more than a year ... to Martha's Vineyard. We'd spent the year before caring for frail, elderly parents who had come to live with us, and this vacation was a precious time for my husband, my two boys, and me to get away. We arrived in a beautiful rented house that we were sharing with close friends early on a Sunday afternoon and had a glorious day and evening together. Early the next morning the phone rang with tragic news. My fifteen-year-old's best friend had been killed in a fall.

The friend who called filled us in with the nightmarish details of Zach jumping from a high rock at a swimming hole our boys frequented, getting his foot caught in a root, and mortally injuring himself on the rocks below. The wake would be held in four days, and the funeral the day after that.

All the pleasure of the preceding day drained from our bodies as we arranged for transportation home and sat, crushed by the news. My friend called back and we talked for a while. Before she hung up she said, "You're going to be on the Vineyard for several days before you come back for the wake. Try to see everything that's beautiful in front of you and live in that moment."

The advice seemed impossible when I first heard it, but it was in fact profoundly wise. There is a value in having a long-range perspective on life, but there is also a value in being able to live in the moment. Buddhists call this practice "mindfulness." I have a friend who worries a great deal about the accidents her kids *might* have. The fact is, if an accident happens — as it did with Zach — we have plenty of time to deal with it. But if we watch our kids with the feeling that any moment might bring a catastrophe, we lose the pleasure of the moment.

Much to our amazement, we were able to spend four days on Martha's Vineyard watching the ocean, the sunset, and all kinds of birds and were actually able to take pleasure in the beauty around us. We thought often of Zach. Our hearts were broken. But we found sanctuary in the moment. There's a skill involved in looking at what's in front of you and finding the gift in it. To some extent we're talking about a "half-full" versus "half-empty" approach to life. But beyond that, this sort of "vision" really cuts away all kinds of clutter.

Principle #6 — Learn to be flexible.

Rigidity is the hobgoblin of an unsatisfying life. Many of us develop patterns of behavior — habits — that take on a life of their own. In fact, there is a real value in change ... in shaking things up every now and then and surprising everyone, including yourself.

The kind of flexibility we're advocating here can be very far-reaching. Think about it in terms of food. How about a baked potato for breakfast? Too tired to make dinner? How about some cold cereal? You may be surprised by the possibilities you uncover once you've learned to loosen up.

Flexibility applies as well to relationships and the expectations we set up within our relationships. Kids often expect their parents to react to things in a certain way and begin to wage battles in anticipation of what they expect. Surprise them. Bend. Think in terms of options rather than in terms of "shoulds."

Finally, allow some flexibility in terms of your expectations. During this period of simplification it's especially valuable to question yourself every time you "take a stand." There are many stands worth taking, but there are also stands that have lost their significance. Only you and the people you care about can be the judge. Keep in mind that there's a fine line between being flexible, being wishy-washy, and being rigid. It's a line worth exploring!

Principle #7 — Prioritize.

Once you've figured out all the things you *must* do and thought about which of those things you most enjoy, you'll be in a position to prioritize.

What activities and things are you able to live without? What activities and things are most important for you preserve? What activities would you like to initiate? The entire notion of prioritizing how you spend your time implies that you actually have some control over your life. It's that kind of control and satisfaction that this book aims to foster.

Clearly, we all have things we must do that we wish we didn't have to do. But, as we said earlier, you'll be surprised to discover just how much choice you have about where your energies go. As you move on to Chapter 2 and begin to keep track of your time, think of your activities in terms of:

• the things that are important and need your urgent personal attention. In other words, things that no one but you can do.

• the things that are important to do but either can be put off for the time being, or can be allocated to someone else.

• the things that aren't all that important in terms of your goals or that someone else can do instead of you.

Remember, you really do have the capacity to make choices. And that is the key to your simpler life!

Logging In for a Simpler Life

In this chapter . . .

- *When Am I Doing It?*
- *What Am I Doing?*
- *How Satisfying/Pleasurable Is It?*
- *How Efficient Am I?*
- *What Role Am I In?*
- *End-of-the-Day Analysis*

Whoever it was that said "time flies when you're having fun" was only half right. The truth is that time flies . . . whether you're having fun or not. Okay, maybe while you're sitting in the endodontist's chair having a root canal it feels as though each second is crawling by, but generally most of us feel that there just aren't enough hours in the day. As a rule, when we crawl into bed at night our sense of satisfaction is rarely commensurate with the amount of energy we've expended just doing all the things we've needed to do to make our way through the day.

The issue of "doing more now and enjoying it less" is, of course, the *raison d'être* for this book; and as we said earlier, we're offering a two-pronged approach to the problem. One of the ways we seek to cope is by organizing, finding shortcuts through daily drudgery, and seeking out helpful hints like those that follow. Beyond that, however, we need to examine precisely what it is that we spend our time doing.

There are twenty-four hours in each day, and if we spend eight of those hours sleeping, we've still got sixteen hours to fill with activity. Before we can think about what we might do to make those sixteen hours at least as satisfying as our eight hours of slumber, we need to take a close look at the activities that occupy our time.

The chapter you are about to read is a workbook chapter. Our goal is to have you create a log that documents exactly what you do with your time. Ideally, the log should cover everything you do over the course of a week. If it becomes too odious a task to cover a week's worth of time, keep the log for one day during the week and one day on the weekend. If you narrow it down to two days, make sure those days are fairly typical.

Take a look at the illustration on page 22 and make a copy of it or put the same headings across the page of a notebook that's small enough to keep in a pocket or purse. You will be making notations in this log all day long, and you need to have it in a readily accessible place.

Now, a word about the headings and what you'll be entering in each column.

When Am I Doing It?

If you've never worn a wristwatch, now is the time to start, because this column on your log requires vigilance. Every time you begin a new activity — shopping, making dinner, putting a child to bed, washing the kitchen floor, or negotiating a multi-million dollar deal — log in your start time. And when you've finished the task at hand, log in your stop time before you move on to something else.

What Am I Doing?

In this column describe your activity. The idea is to be as thorough and specific as you can. "Getting washed, dressed, and ready to leave," for example, is likely to be most people's first entry. If, however, you spend fifteen minutes looking for the keys to the car, or for the work you did the night before, or for a pair of panty hose that don't have a run in them, make sure to log it as a separate entry. In fact, it wouldn't be a bad idea, the first time you "log in," to break down your broad, basic categories into lots of small ones: keep track of how much time you spend picking out clothing; putting on makeup; making breakfast (for yourself and for others); packing lunch.

Another example of a broad category might be "driving to work." If you stop at the gas station to fill the gas tank, make it a separate entry. If you spend fifteen minutes clearing snow off the windshield, enter that as well. What we're looking for are the glitches. The things that will make you say, when you review your log later in the day, "I can't believe I spent so much time doing *that!*"

If you spend your day in a workplace, be sure to keep track of things such as phone time (both personal and work-related), meetings, daydreaming, eating, and shmoozing. Obviously, the break-down of a work day will be very different depending on the workplace. Nurses, teachers, secretaries, salespeople, and mechanics all have very different work environments, and those differences will be reflected in their logs.

Regardless of whether you work outside the home or in the home, there will undoubtedly be several entries that involve home maintenance. Again, rather than having a general entry for "cleaning," try to be specific: for example, "vacuuming," "windows," "toilets," "fridge." And when it comes to downtime be specific as well. "Relaxing" won't tell you as much when it comes time to analyze your log as will "watching TV" or "reading" or "listening to music."

How Satisfying/ Pleasurable Is It?

Some of the things we spend our time doing can be talked about in terms of pleasure. If you draw yourself a bath with wonderful oils, light a dozen candles, turn on some soft music, and settle in for an hour, you're probably aiming for a pleasurable experience.

There are other things we do that aren't really pleasurable but are, nonetheless, quite satisfying. For example, I find it satisfying to clean out my refrigerator. I don't enjoy the task, per se, but I enjoy the sense of accomplishment when I've cleared the vegetable bin of moldy zucchini and wiped the shelves clean of spilled yogurt and chocolate syrup. That sense of satisfaction is rekindled each time I open the refrigerator door for the first day or so after I've cleaned it.

The key to logging in regarding pleasure and satisfaction is to understand that this column will be entirely different for different people. There are those who find no pleasure at all in the idea of soaking in a hot tub of water. For them, a quick shower might seem much more enjoyable. And, much to my amazement, there are people who find it much more satisfying to vacuum or clean the toilet than to clean out the refrigerator.

One of the goals of this book is to encourage you to take the time to think about what it is you enjoy doing, and what it is that gives you a sense of satisfaction. The key to reaching that that understanding is to recognize that you are unique. Don't worry about the fact that everyone you know loves to read long Russian novels if, every time you try one, you fall asleep. There are no bonus points in life for suffering through what other people say you should enjoy.

We are suggesting that you rate your pleasure/ satisfaction experience on a scale of one to ten — even though we recognize how difficult that can be. Think of a ten as the most pleasurable/satisfying, and a one as the least, and don't worry about being absolutely accurate. Your idea of a nine may not be the same as someone else's, but you're the only one who matters! When you finish an activity, jot down your pleasure/satisfaction level. Do it quickly. Don't spend too much time thinking about it. Your gut reaction is what matters most, and you don't want to lose it with too much intellectualizing.

How Efficient Am I?

There are times when efficiency is very important. At other times, however, it doesn't figure into the equation at all. Listening to music, for example, is a great and satisfying simple pleasure. It can be your dessert at the end of an otherwise bland, humdrum day, and the issue of efficiency doesn't figure in to the experience at all. When you log in these tasks, simply write NA (not applicable) in the column for efficiency.

Putting your child to bed is less clear-cut. Some people like the idea of an efficient bedtime routine: bath, story, back-rub, song, and out-the-door. Other people, however, take a less efficient approach to bedtime: bath, story, back-rub, song, story, back-rub, listen to music, back-rub and . . . wake up in your child's bed a few hours later. Efficient? No. But pleasurable? Very likely. On tasks like these, you have to weigh whether or not efficiency is of value to you. The decision is entirely personal. There is no "right" or "wrong." If the issue of efficiency does not apply, again, simply enter NA in the column.

Finally, there are tasks in which efficiency is

clearly of great value. If you've ever gone to the market, come home, started to prepare dinner, and discovered that you're missing half the ingredients, you know just what we're talking about. Grocery shopping, food preparation, cleaning, errand hopping, laundry, and many other tasks might be considerably more pleasurable if we did them more efficiently. And if efficiency doesn't make them more pleasurable, it will at least get us through the drudgery more quickly.

So, when you sign off from each task on your log, make a note of how efficiently you think you did it. Again, don't give this too much thought. We don't want your log to take up too much time. Just think in terms of one–ten, with ten being "most efficient."

What Role Am I In?

Most of us wear lots of different hats. We're mothers, fathers, nurses, teachers, homemakers, plumbers, cooks, chauffeurs, lovers, sons and daughters, and lots of other things as well. Our time is filled with responsibilities and activities that accompany each of the roles we play, and it can be very helpful, when we look at how we fill our day, to examine how much time each of our roles consumes.

Before you begin to log in your day, think about the roles you'll be playing. But don't write down your role while you're busy getting through the day. This column and the next — End-of-the-Day Analysis — should be filled in before you go to sleep at night.

End-of-the-Day Analysis

Every night, when you're ready to turn out the light, make the last entries in your log and allow yourself a few minutes to look over your day. The purpose of the log is to give you an opportunity to see where your time goes, and to think about what you would most like to change.

Now is the time to fill in which "role" you were playing while you were engaged in each activity. As you do that, check out the pleasure/satisfaction column and notice the correlation. Which roles offered you the most satisfaction? Which offered the least? What might you do to allow more time for the activities that give you the greatest pleasure/ satisfaction payback? If your spouse is keeping a log, check with him or her. Maybe you can do some juggling that will leave you both feeling more satisfied.

This is also a good time to see where you invest most of your time. Add up the time you spend in each role. What role consumes the bulk of your day? Now, take a look at the pleasure/satisfaction column. How does your most time-consuming role correlate with your sense of satisfaction and plea- sure? Obviously, people who feel best about their days have a very high correlation between the roles that consume most of their time and the activities that give them the greatest pleasure or satisfaction. As you attempt to simplify your life and increase your sense of satisfaction, you should shoot for precisely that kind of correlation.

The end-of-the-day analysis is also the time to ask yourself what most surprised you about your activities that day. Perhaps you found that the time you spent chauffeuring the kids was actually pleasant because it gave you a quiet opportunity to talk. Maybe you're surprised by how much time you spend doing things you don't enjoy at all. Or maybe you've discovered that you enjoy chores that other people complain about. Jot these observations down in the last column.

Keep track of your activities for a week, using a new sheet each day. When the week is over, set aside some time to review it. Notice what you found most satisfying and pleasurable. Read through the **Seven Guiding Principles** again and reflect upon how you can apply them to what you've observed about your week.

Here's a recap:

#1 Relax your standards.

#2 Free yourself of stereotypical roles.

#3 Take time to figure out what you find most satisfying.

#4 Create time for the things you care about.

#5 Learn to enjoy what's in front of you.

#6 Learn to be flexible.

#7 Prioritize.

There are, to be sure, things we simply must do every day, but we have more control over our time than we think . . . and we most definitely have the potential to change the way we do things.

Read on for ways to cut the time spent on those chores or to make them more enjoyable. And as for the things that rank highest? *Make* time for them. You're the only one who can.

Keeping Life Simple: Daily Log

When Am I Doing It?	What Am I Doing?	How Satisfying/ Pleasurable Is It?	How Efficient Am I?	What Role Am I In?

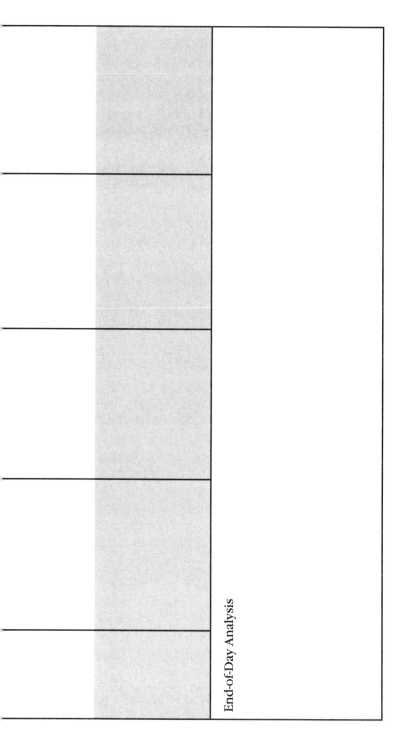

End-of-Day Analysis

Simple Satisfactions

In this chapter . . .

- *Rest and Relaxation*
- *Gardening*
- *Taking Care of Yourself*
- *Person to Person*
- *Pleasurable Pastimes for Grownups*
- *Family Pleasures*
- *Edible Delights*

I t's not a new notion — "the best things in life are free" — but it's an easy one to lose sight of. For one thing, the entire advertising industry tells us that we need all kinds of bells and whistles to make our lives meaningful. Are you interested in walking? You'll need special shoes. Are you interested in tennis? You'll need to understand the technology of graphite, aluminum, fiberglass, gut, nylon, shock absorbers, and much, much more. Even before you can put your hands into the earth to dig a garden you may feel the need to buy special pants with knee pads, tools inspired by ancient Japanese gardening lore, chemicals, nonchemicals, stone animals, gazing balls, Japanese beetle traps, invisible fences, weed whackers, straw hats, weeping hoses, an endless number of how-to books, and catalogs full of STUFF.

Beyond the problem of constantly having glitsy, indispensable carrots dangled in front of us, we tend to lose sight of simple satisfactions because we're so busy running around. When you're racing in your car from one meeting to another, you don't always think to sit down in a comfortable chair and listen to your favorite music. And when you're trudging into the house carrying bags of groceries after carting kids from basketball practice to ballet, you sometimes forget to look up and notice a spectacular, inspiring night sky.

What follows are reminders. Most especially, this chapter is a reminder to stop and think about what you enjoy that's readily accessible. The log you completed in Chapter 2 will be of value as you make your way through the pages that follow. Look at the things you most enjoyed and think about which of those things fall into this category. In the meantime, pour yourself some tea, coffee, hot chocolate, wine — whatever *you* like — and enjoy what you're about to read. It's your time to relax.

Rest and Relaxation

Your master bedroom should be inviting, serene, and maybe even sensual. To that end, make your bed in the morning, put your clothing away (or at least behind a closed closet door), and remind yourself that you have a right to close the door behind you. (Your children, by the way, should have the same right to a closed door.)

Keep a good book, some relaxing tapes, lotion, and a pad and pencil near your bed. You may wake up from a dream that is well worth writing down!

Observant Jews celebrate the Sabbath every week by not driving, not using electrical appliances, and not answering the phone. It is truly a day of rest. Try it out for yourself; you'll be surprised by how renewed you feel at the end of the day. Turn on your answering machine, go for a walk or a bike ride, play some non-electronic games with your family, sing, make music, or read the entire newspaper cover to cover.

You can save money and develop a new appreciation for your home and neighborhood by taking a vacation without going anywhere. The key, however, is to be very strict about the fact that you are on vacation. This is not a time to get lots of chores done. In fact, if you don't have cleaning help, this might be a time to hire someone to come in. The key is to relax and enjoy the surroundings you work so hard to provide: listen to your favorite music, sit on your deck, read your favorite books, sleep late, and take lots of long, long walks. By the end of the vacation you should be able to say, "Now I remember why I live where I do!"

><.—0—.—<

There are points in this book where we urge you to hire help. Here, however, it's important to evaluate when it makes sense to do the things yourself. Sometimes the issue is economics. At other times, however, you really need to assess your experience with the task at hand. If planing and nailing wood gives you a sense of satisfaction, then make time to do it yourself ... even if you can make more money using your time otherwise and hiring a carpenter to do your woodwork.

><.—0—.—<

Walking is good, but hiking can be thrilling ... especially if there are hikes in your area that culminate with a great view. Go to the local library and ask for a book on local hikes. Then, wait for a good day and head out. It's free for the taking.

><.—0—.—<

If you live in an area that experiences real winters, buy yourself a set of flannel sheets. You'll begin to eagerly anticipate crawling into bed at about 4:00 PM.

To the right, books; to the left, a tea-cup. In front of me, the fireplace; behind me, the post. There is no greater happiness than this.

Tiega

There's something special about sitting around a fire. If you've got a fireplace, use it. If you don't, wait for a beautiful summer night and make a campfire in your backyard. Check out the stars while you're at it.

⊳┼◦┼◦┼◦┼◃

Bake bread. Sure, you need the luxury of time to do this, but consider it on a Saturday or Sunday . . . and don't use one of those bread machines. You want to get your hands into the dough, work out some frustrations, watch it rise, punch it down, and then relax and enjoy the sweet smell while it bakes. Which is to say nothing of the ultimate treat of putting the finished product into your mouth!

⊳┼◦┼◦┼◦┼◃

Give yourself a half hour at the end of the day to unwind by doing whatever feels relaxing to you: reading, listening to music, meditating, and so on.

⊳┼◦┼◦┼◦┼◃

Bird watching is a great hobby. Get a few books about your feathered friends and the homes they build for themselves. Then look around outside. It's particularly fun to hook up with others in your area who are interested in birds and check things out together.

⊳┼◦┼◦┼◦┼◃

Support public radio. The best deal in the world is an annual contribution to your nearest public radio station. For whatever you're inclined to give — and, in light of federal cutbacks, you should try to give as much as you can — you'll get countless hours of wonderful news and entertainment programming. Do it!

If you enjoy wind chimes, buy a really good set. You don't want to hear a lot of clunking noises every time the wind blows.

⊱────◦────⊰

There is something about lying in a hammock, especially if it's hung between two great shade trees, that makes it impossible to do anything other than relax. Hammocks are very pricey these days, so check out yard sales for a bargain.

⊱────◦────⊰

Think about stenciling a wall or learning how to do marbleizing, sponging, or texturing. There are lots of books on these techniques, as well as pamphlets you can pick up at your local paint shop. It's both simple and satisfying.

⊱────◦────⊰

Buy yourself some flowers. They'll brighten up your day, and aside from that, it's fun to do something nice for yourself!

⊱────◦────⊰

Send flowers to a good friend for no special reason. It's great to surprise people with something nice . . . especially since most surprises are unpleasant.

⊱────◦────⊰

There's nothing quite so satisfying as getting a great bargain. Of course, bargains don't come knocking at your door. You've got to go out and find them. Tag sales, thrift shops, end-of-season sales, used sporting equipment stores, newspaper ads, and friends who are looking to dump some stuff . . . that's where you begin.

Every now and then splurge a little . . . it's only a little . . . and buy a tin of exotic imported tea. It can be English, Indian, or Chinese. You'll find the excitement of the taste will give you a real lift in an otherwise routine day. And when you're finished with the tea, the handsome tins make useful receptacles in which you can organize anything from tacks to nails to . . . ordinary tea bags.

▻┈◈┈◅

Try to stay focused on the present. Remember the old adage: "The past is history, the future a mystery, but today is a gift, which is why it is called the Present."

▻┈◈┈◅

Clean your car. There's something pleasurable about driving around in a shiny, freshly vacuumed car. Do it yourself in your own driveway, visit a do-it-yourself car wash, or pull through the drive-in. However it gets done, it's worth the effort. And don't forget to polish up the vinyl dash.

▻┈◈┈◅

Take five minutes to relax your back, neck, and facial muscles. Most of us carry tension in these areas. All you need to do is focus on these areas one at a time, and as you exhale, try consciously to relax that part of your body. Concentrate on one shoulder at a time. Pay particular attention to your jaws, cheeks, and forehead.

▻┈◈┈◅

Try to write a country song. You can do it best if you're on a long car trip by yourself. It that doesn't work, try taking a steamy shower. Everyone and everything sounds great in the shower.

Have a massage, if you can afford to get one. If not, take a few classes with your partner or a good friend, and then do it for each other.

Although I'm categorically against clutter, there's something very satisfying about collecting. Find something that appeals to your sense of fancy that's also inexpensive, and begin a collection. Matchbooks, tea cups, old sporting goods, birds' nests . . . whatever.

If you've got a baby, forget about those baby bathtubs and run a nice deep tub for yourself and your little one. Sit with your knees up and put your baby on your tummy, with his back against your thighs and his feet across your chest. This is a pleasurable, intimate time and especially great for dads, who miss out on the intimacy of nursing.

Help yourself to relax by practicing square breathing. Breathe in to the count of four, hold it for the count of four, exhale for the count of four and pause for the count of four. Now do it all again . . . and again . . . and again.

Greet a neighbor. If someone new moves onto your block, make it a point to go over and say hello. You might even stop by with a box of cookies. Even if you tend to be shy, this kind of welcoming act can be as wonderful for the person who's doing it as it is for the person on the receiving end. Remember, we're not talking about a life-long commitment of friendship. Simply a welcome.

Keep a cheap pair of lawn chairs in the trunk of your car. You never know when you'll pass a beautiful meadow or a wonderful old graveyard that beckons you to come and sit for a while.

Plan an afternoon with your children on an "Adventure into the Unknown." Think of three or four places that they've never been. Ideally, these places should not cost money, although if a museum is included there may be a small admission fee. You needn't stay long at any one place — or you can linger. There is no schedule. Remember . . . this is an adventure. Places to think about include: airports, tall office buildings, parks, factories, and museums. It can be an adventure into family history if you include "Where Grandma and Grandpa lived when they were kids," and "Where Mom and Dad lived when we were kids." See if any local artists have "open studio" hours. Remember ... this is a magical mystery tour, not a trip to the mall.

Unless your religion forbids it, consider becoming an organ donor. Living with the knowledge that your death might save another's life feels good.

Check out a few books on tape from your public library for the car trip to and from work.

Unless you will cause someone a great deal of distress, exchange a gift that doesn't delight you. The point is for you to love what you have, and whoever gave it to you will probably feel even more strongly about that than we do!

Try out the music your parents listened to when they were your age. You may have a wonderful surprise in store!

›—‹•›—‹—•—‹—•—‹‹

Nothing is more economical and soul-satisfying than starting a new plant from an old one. Simply clip off a healthy leaf-and-stem from a mother plant, stick it in some moist rooting medium in an old cottage cheese container, cover with plastic wrap, keep in a warm place away from bright light, and soon you'll have a plantlet with roots. When this happens, remove the plastic wrap and set the plantlet on a bright windowsill as the new leaves develop. When several have formed, you can plant it up in a clay pot with some good soil.

›—‹•›—‹—•—‹—•—‹‹

Hosting a block party is a way to get to know your neighbors.

›—‹•›—‹—•—‹—•—‹‹

Wood-burning saunas don't cost much to build, and the psychic benefits are enormous.

›—‹•›—‹—•—‹—•—‹‹

Read aloud to children, your own or someone else's. Many elementary teachers welcome volunteers, and it's a fun way to spend time with kids.

The art of art, the glory of expression and the sunshine of the light of letters, is simplicity.

Walt Whitman (1819–1892)

Listen. It's easy to fall into the habit of listening to what other people have to say only so you can come up with a response. Try listening in a genuinely open way. You'll probably hear something interesting.

↦┈◆┈◅

If you've never "forced" bulbs, you're in for one of life's truly simple treats. For about $2 or $3, buy a few paperwhite narcissus bulbs. Pot them up in gravel or soil and put them in a cool dark place for a few weeks. Then bring them into the light and water sparingly until shoots appear, and when you have a fabulous paperwhite narcissus bloom in the middle of the winter it will be more thrilling than a $50 bouquet.

↦┈◆┈◅

Take your dog for a good long walk.

↦┈◆┈◅

When you go for a walk, try to listen to the sounds around you. I hope you'll hear something more than traffic.

↦┈◆┈◅

Enjoy your sense of smell. Sometimes we're so busy running from place to place that we don't allow ourselves to enjoy the good smells around us. In fact, the part of our brain that controls smell is the same part that controls memory and emotions . . . which is why a certain smell can trigger a flood of feelings and memories. Smell the bread baking, the coffee, the grass, the baby's neck, and anything else that makes you feel good. The good feeling will last a lifetime.

Find a moment every day to reflect on what you have to be grateful about. It's very easy to be overwhelmed by what's difficult in our lives ... and we all have problems at one point or another. But sometimes those difficulties cloud the good things in our lives. In fact, sometimes you need to look at other people's difficulties to appreciate what you've got going for yourself.

⊱⋆⊰

Try to have an enjoyable activity in mind for when you have unexpected time. Make it something you really enjoy doing that requires very little preparation or planning (i.e., a walk, a short workout, a magazine, a cup of soup). If your dental appointment has been canceled or a business lunch falls through, use that time as a gift to yourself and fill it with one of your "easily accessible enjoyable activities."

⊱⋆⊰

If you've spent the last twenty-five years or so avoiding your college or high school reunion, you might want to rethink it. These gatherings are never what you anticipate and usually offer lots of food for thought.

⊱⋆⊰

Make it a point to get outside as often as possible. We often structure our days so that we only go out of doors in order to get to the car and to go from the car to a building. Being outside just for the pleasure of being in the natural world is very nourishing. A ten minute walk, even if it is only around the block, done for no purpose (I'm not talking here about power walking!) can be a time of renewal.

Try keeping a journal of your thoughts. It will feel luxurious while you're doing it, as well as in the years to come.

~·~◦~·~

If you're a person who takes pleasure in gardening, try pressing flowers. There are lots of good books that will show you how.

~·~◦~·~

Go to your local historical society or library and learn about the area in which you live. Knowing about local history makes all aspects of your life more meaningful.

~·~◦~·~

Take a bubble bath or a bath with some wonderfully fragrant oils. You might also want to light a dozen votive candles and buy a copy of *Chant*. Talk about a spiritual experience!

~·~◦~·~

Throw your towels or terry robe in the dryer before you get into the tub and ask someone to bring them to you when you're ready to get out. Heated towels. Mmmm!

~·~◦~·~

Think about the activities that give you the most pleasure. Sometimes, if you really allow yourself to get lost in the thought, it's almost as good as being there.

~·~◦~·~

Snow days can be a source of frustration or the opportunity for unscheduled time at home. Give up and enjoy them.

Make a wish list. Write down things you'd love to do or have. Safari? Paris? Theater? Don't worry about how outrageous the list is. It's absolutely private and it doesn't cost a cent. Even if you never get to do the things on the list, you can enjoy the fantasy.

———○———

Don't speed . . . even if you're in a hurry. In fact, slow down a bit. It will give you a chance to enjoy what's around you, and make your trip feel a bit more relaxed.

———○———

Visit the neighborhood in which you grew up.

———○———

Step outside before you're ready to go to bed and look up. It's quite extraordinary, and it will help you put every aspect of your life in perspective.

———○———

Watch the sun set. Does this sound corny? Think again. There's no light show as inspiring as the one "up there." Stop and look. It's worth the time.

———○———

Do nothing. We tend to think of time as something that must be used productively. It's also important, however, to allow yourself time to "veg out." Actually, you may be surprised by how restorative (and consequently productive) that kind of time can be.

———○———

Go on a mini-retreat, alone or with a friend, at a bird or wildlife sanctuary. Pack a picnic lunch and spend the day.

Sing! Not long ago a group of friends came over and one of them brought sheet music: Rodgers and Hart, Cole Porter, Gershwin, all kinds of old standards we knew but didn't know we knew. One friend sat down to play and we all gathered round for what turned out to be the most fun we'd had in years. Talk is great, but when you're gathered around a piano doing three-part harmony there's a real impulse to put your arm around a friend. It feels good . . . even when it isn't all that harmonious.

Go to your local library and check out some CDs that offer a kind of music you don't ordinarily hear. Native American flute music, for example, might open up new vistas for someone who hasn't heard it before. It did for me.

Give someone an unexpected gift. It can be as satisfying to the giver as it is to the recipient. This can be especially true when you give the gift to someone whose contributions or efforts often go unacknowledged. Meet your child's school bus on a stormy day with flowers for the driver. Give your secretary a box of candy . . . just because. It'll make your day.

Think of things that you've always done the same way and try, instead, to wander down an alternate path. That might mean a new kind of cuisine, a different kind of music or book, or even a big move.

Indulge yourself with an hour of doing nothing but listening to your favorite music.

Find some quiet time to think . . . about where you are in life, about your goals, about your disappointments, and so on. Insight can be very curative and energizing, but it requires thought.

⊷—◦—⊷

Use cloth napkins. They feel good and add a special feeling to most meals. They're also much more earth-friendly than "disposable" paper.

⊷—◦—⊷

Give yourself a small task that you know you will be able to begin and complete in a satisfying way. Pick a small cabinet in your bathroom to clean out. Organize a drawer. The key is to allow yourself the satisfaction of getting a job done.

⊷—◦—⊷

Keep downtime sacred and don't feel guilty about it. If you're lying around watching TV with your kids, don't feel guilty about not working.

⊷—◦—⊷

Buy a few scented geraniums for your home. They're easy to care for, and when you brush their leaves they release wonderful fragrances of mint, lemon, rose, orange, nutmeg, and more.

The least of things with a meaning is worth more in life than the greatest of things without it.

Carl Jung (1875–1961)

Even if you don't meditate, you can practice one of meditation's most valuable lessons: do only what you are doing, be only where you are. In other words, don't let your mind take you to everything else that needs to be done, or changed, or remembered. If you are driving to work, focus on driving to work — not on the fight you had with your child the night before, or the memory of how you embarrassed yourself twenty years ago. This isn't easy, but it's well worth the effort.

Gardening

Stop mowing your lawn and plant a meadow. Lots of mail-order catalogs sell wonderful combinations of mixed wildflower seeds. Select an area of your lawn and plant a sweet-smelling maintenance-free meadow. It takes some work to establish it, but the rewards are worth it.

Plant a cutting garden near enough to the house for you to step out every day and cut some fresh flowers. These gardens can include zinnias, dahlias, gladioli, and whatever else strikes your fancy.

Make an indoor winter herb garden. Enjoy fresh herbs all winter long, as well as the pleasure of watching them grow. Best choices for an indoor garden include basil, bay, chives, mint, parsley, and thyme. Pots should be clay and a minimum of 6 inches across to ensure adequate growing room. You'll need a window with a southern or western exposure that offers 4 to 6 hours of light, or a fluorescent light. Put the pots in a tray lined with stones and a small amount of water to provide adequate moisture. Use the fresh herbs when you cook. If you become overloaded, dry them by placing them in the oven. Once they're dried, crumble them up and store them in an air-tight jar. You might even want to experiment with different herb mixtures.

⊱──◦──◦──⊰

Share plants. Part of the joy of gardening is its conviviality. "Plant people" like to share, and it certainly beats paying nursery prices. You might even consider setting up a plant exchange in your area through a local agricultural cooperative. Keep in mind that when you invite people to come and "thin" your garden, it's as good for your garden as it is for the people who go home with your perennials.

⊱──◦──◦──⊰

Make compost. There's a definite pleasure in doing something good for the earth, and recycling kitchen wastes is an easy way for you to contribute. It also simplifies your life by making less smelly garbage to haul to a waste station. All vegetable matter can be recycled, including tea bags, coffee grounds and filters, paper towels used to clean up kitchen spills, and, of course, all vegetable and fruit parings. Don't compost any meat or dairy products. Also, remember that you don't need a fancy com-poster. A compost heap can be precisely that . . . a heap somewhere in the corner of your yard. Buy a good book on composting for all the details, and find out whether your community has a commu-nity compost pile.

Taking Care of Yourself

Avoid using a doctor with whom you don't feel entirely comfortable. Even when everyone tells you that he/she is the best, if your doctor is not a person with whom you can relax and have a leisurely, relaxed conversation about your health, he/she isn't the doctor for you.

Make it a point to have a physical examination once a year. If you've been avoiding it, chances are you're worried about something. And the worry will show itself one way or another. Get the physical and breathe a sigh of relief.

Give yourself a breast exam.

To prevent eyestrain, keep your computer screen clean. Follow instructions that came with your monitor for cleaning the screen.

Nothing complicates life more than back pain. According to the American Academy of Orthopedic Surgeons, lower back pain is second only to the common cold as a cause of lost work days. The best ways to avoid back pain include:

• Unlock and bend your knees when lifting or leaning forward. Keep objects close to your body and directly in front of you.

• Avoid excessive reaching in front of you or overhead. Use a stool rather than reaching up.

• Stop smoking, especially if you have a smoker's cough. Coughing puts pressure on spinal discs.

- Don't sit for more than thirty minutes at a time without taking a standing or walking break. Also, shift positions if you've been standing for a long period of time.
- Keep your chair close to your desk or table.
- Eat right and exercise.
- Sleep on a mattress that allows lower back muscles to relax.

Avoid back and neck tension at your desk. If you work in front of a computer, the following are absolutely critical:

- The screen is at eye level.
- You keep your elbows at a 90° angle.
- You keep your feet flat on the floor.
- You avoid glare on the screen from a window or light.
- You get up and stretch for five minutes every hour.
- You invest in a good desk chair.

Walking, jogging, biking, or working out regularly on a home exercise machine can have a positive impact on your physical and emotional health. Do it . . . even if you don't think you have time for it. It's good for the body . . . good for the mind . . . good for the soul . . . and it doesn't have to cost a cent.

Walk with a friend. It's a perfect way to do two things at once: exercise and create an opportunity for intimacy.

Ride a bicycle, if you can, to commute to and from work or to do other errands. You'll accomplish two goals at once: you'll be exercising at the same time as you're saving money on gas and making the earth just a bit less polluted.

In addition to a regular exercise program, get extra exercise by sprinting up a flight of steps rather than using an elevator.

Most people would agree that other than genes, diet is a key factor in health. Keep in mind the seven basic principles for developing and maintaining a healthier diet developed by the United States Department of Health and Human Services together with the Department of Agriculture:

- Eat a variety of foods.
- Maintain a desirable weight.
- Avoid too much fat, saturated fat, and cholesterol.
- Eat foods with adequate starch and fiber.
- Avoid too much sugar.
- Avoid too much salt.
- If you consume alcoholic beverages, do so in moderation.

Ours is a sleep-deprived culture. Are you getting all the sleep you need? Keep in mind that sleep triggers a growth hormone to renew tissues, form new red blood cells, and promote bone formation. Beyond that, sleep enables you to dream; and dreaming is an essential emotional outlet. If you aren't getting enough sleep, chances are you're irritable and less able to concentrate. Assign yourself a regular bedtime and allow yourself a good half hour to get ready.

Develop a sleep ritual that involves doing the same thing every night before you get into bed. If you do the same things in the same order each night, you're more likely to have a restful sleep.

Before you go to sleep at night, lie in bed and try the following relaxation exercise, working your way up your body. Begin by saying "Relax my toes," and make a conscious effort to relax them. "Relax my arch," and do it. "Relax my ankle," and continue all the way up to your forehead. Don't miss any area . . . they're probably all filled with tension.

Replace your innerspring and mattress if they are eight to ten years old. A mattress that is too soft can interfere with the quality of your sleep.

It is vain to say human beings ought to be satisfied with tranquillity: they must have action; and they will make it if they cannot find it.

Charlotte Brontë (1816–1855)

If you have trouble sleeping, try the following:

- Eat something high in carbohydrates (such as pasta or bread).

- Sip warm milk or herbal tea (make sure it's decaffinated).

- Take a warm bath.

- Alternately tense and relax your muscles.

- Breathe deeply.

- Get up and read or listen to music.

- Try self-hypnosis ("I am getting sleepy ... ").

- Make up a poem.

- Stop trying to sleep.

- Think about whether you're getting too much sleep.

Cut down on caffeine. If you consume too much caffeine, either from coffee, tea, chocolate, or cola beverages, it will interfere with the quality of your deep sleep. Smoking and alcohol have similar effects on sleep.

Although regular exercise is very important, it's never a good idea to exercise too close to bedtime. It can be too stimulating and interfere with your sleep.

If you wake up in the middle of the night, anxious about all that awaits you in the day to come, get up and write a list for yourself. There! It's on paper. Now go back to sleep.

Warm milk is a natural tranquilizer. Calcium helps you relax. Try a glass at night before you go to bed. Drink skim milk if you're worried about calories, but it's a great way to usher in the Sandman and ward off osteoporosis at the same time.

⊷

You don't need fancy astringents to soothe your tired eyes. Instead, put two wet used tea bags in the freezer for a couple of minutes while you gently rub some cooking oil over your eyelids. Take the tea bags out and put them on your lids for about fifteen minutes.

Person to Person

Make a dinner date with your "significant other" at least once a month. If you get together with friends, that's fine. But if not, make it a point to go out together to someplace where you can sit and talk without any other responsibilities.

⊷

Take up a hobby with your partner, something that interests both of you. Join a choir; take a computer or cooking class; study Chinese; take up bird watching, ballroom dancing, or bowling. You'll meet new people and have new things to talk about when you have your dinner date together.

⊷

Find quality time to spend with friends. This means scheduling a time to spend together and sticking to it — even if it's just an hour of sipping tea and talking.

It's important to make time for your children. When you walk into the house at the end of the day, they will feel that they have a right to your attention . . . and they're correct. Don't entertain phone calls while your three-year-old is tugging at your trousers. Turn on the answering machine and allocate a set amount of time that will be exclusively theirs.

———◆———

Do your absolute best to get along with your in-laws. If you genuinely like them, that shouldn't be difficult. Even if you don't, it takes more effort to battle with them than it does to find a way to coexist. When the going gets rough just remind yourself that they must have done something right . . . after all, they managed to turn out the person with whom you are spending your life.

———◆———

Never make public statements, confrontations, or write anything down in the heat of passion. Whatever you're feeling is fine. You needn't make judgments about it. But you need to respect yourself enough to allow time to cool down before you show yourself to the world.

———◆———

Make it a point to share a good feeling you might have with your kids, your spouse, your friends, and your co-workers.

———◆———

The better you are at networking, the simpler your life will be. By "networking," we're talking about a process of connecting with people to whom you might be helpful and who might be helpful to you. Keep in mind that the concept of networking applies equally to personal things and to the world of business. If your child is interested in gymnastics, for example, you'll need to network with the parents of other children who share that interest unless you plan to spend your life chauffeuring your child.

Make it a point to schedule time for intimacy. If you and your partner always get into bed exhausted, the days and weeks will fly by without much contact. But if you plan, quite deliberately, to get into bed an hour early, light a candle, and turn on some music, you'll have the time to enjoy each other . . . and remember how nice that is.

Pleasurable Pastimes for Grownups

Local theater groups offer all kinds of opportunities for inexpensive fun. For starters, if you have any interest at all in theater (be it as an actor or a techie), join. It's a great way to meet people. If you're not interested in participating, don't miss the performances. They're usually affordable and entertaining.

Find something you want to learn about — a period in history, a person, a kind of art, an aspect of home repair, how to build a wooden canoe, how to play a recorder, how to knit — and become an expert on it.

Play an instrument. Remember those piano/violin/saxophone lessons your mother made you take when you were young? Music lessons might be an entirely different experience this time around!

Learn a foreign language. Use the time in your car to do this. There are many taped programs that really work.

Dance. People have always found joy in moving their bodies to the beat of good music. Whether you prefer folk dancing, contra dancing, square dancing, ballroom dancing, African dancing, or jazzercize, do it with someone you like.

Revisit the religion you grew up with. You may find it comforting to say a prayer before you go to sleep, attend a mass, or kiss a mezuzah before you enter your home.

Get involved in a political campaign. It can be local, state, or federal, but grassroots involvement in politics is what keeps our democracy going. And there's a real sense of satisfaction in that . . . even if you lose.

Write letters to friends and family. There's something special — leisurely and thoughtful — about the way people communicate on paper. Take the time to do it. You'll learn something about yourself in the process.

If you love to cook good food, find some other people who share your passion and get together once a month (or however often suits you) to create and share in a grand dining experience.

⊷⊶⊙⊷⊶

If you love coffee, treat yourself to really good coffee rather than hot, dark liquid. The best way to get the most out of a cup of coffee is to:

• Grind your own beans and enjoy the aroma.

• Use good water to make your coffee.

• Keep the ratio of water to coffee at 2 tablespoons of grounds for each 6-ounce cup of water.

• Use a nice cup, and heat it (rinse it with hot water) before you pour in the coffee.

• If you like milk in your coffee, take an extra minute to heat the milk. If you allow it to froth just a bit and then pour it into the coffee, you'll really notice the difference.

• Drink your coffee within 15 to 20 minutes of the time you brew it. After that, it will begin to lose its flavor.

• Never reheat or boil coffee. Keep it hot by pouring it into a vacuum thermos.

• Store coffee beans in the freezer.

⊷⊶⊙⊷⊶

Every New Year's I write a long letter to a friend telling her about my year. Other than that letter we rarely talk, but the annual communication has become important to us both. This year she wrote, "I have kept your letters for the last sixteen years and as I read them now they come together, in a very beautiful way, to make a life. Thank you."

Get a tree identification book and find out what's growing in your backyard.

Take a Sunday afternoon nap.

Learn the Japanese art of origami. It's easy, inexpensive, and enormously satisfying.

Knitting really is a simple pleasure . . . a sort of mantra for your fingers with a wonderful gift at the end!

Think about a book that you absolutely loved when you were in college, and reread it. Great literature is every bit as great the second time around.

Reading groups have grown in popularity. One of the pleasures of reading is talking about what you've read. Gather a group of people and meet on a regular basis. You can each take a turn selecting the book that you come together to discuss. You make the rules. The key is to have fun. There are several good books on how to organize and maintain a reading group. Look for one at your local library.

Keep the book you never get to read either in the car or in your purse. If you're waiting in a long line at the supermarket, or if you're caught waiting for a tardy child, it will become an opportunity to read.

If you aren't already addicted to used book stores, find one to get lost in and you'll keep going back. The books are usually very reasonably priced, you'll get the pleasure of reading hardcover instead of paperback, and you'll have an afternoon's worth of entertainment just browsing.

Don't forget the public library. It's free. Moreover, you won't accumulate shelves and shelves of books to pack and move and dust and, let's face it, rarely read for a second time.

Family Pleasures

If there's one near you, join a CSA — Community Supported Agriculture. This wonderful movement benefits everyone involved. Local people buy shares in the farm and, in return, enjoy a share of the farm's produce for most of the year; this enables small farmers to thrive and subscribers to get an incredible buy on organic veggies. As an added bonus, there are no supermarket lines and none of the labor involved in making your own garden.

Go out and buy three new decks of playing cards and keep them in a specific drawer. You'll need three because many card games require two . . . and chances are you'll need a deck from which to pull replacement cards. Now, enjoy playing cards. It's great fun that adults and children can share.

> *The price we pay for the complexity of life is too high. When you think of all the effort you have to put in — telephonic, technological, and relational — to alter even the slightest bit of behavior in this strange world we call social life, you are left pining for the straightforwardness of primitive peoples and their physical work.*
>
> **Jean Baudrillard (1929–)**

The simplest and deepest joys often come from spending time with children. Quality time shrinks, though, when our lives are cluttered with meetings, errands, phone calls. Some parents limit themselves to one evening meeting per week; others schedule all evening meetings during the first week of the month so that they have a long stretch of time at home. Try dropping one committee and dedicating that time to family activities. It's a cliché, but it's still true that they're only young once.

＞—◆◇—◆—◇

Talk with your children! They have a lot of interesting things to say, and the more they think you're interested, the more interesting they'll be.

＞—◆◇—◆—◇

When you put your children to bed, don't ask them how their day was. It's much too general a question for them to answer in a meaningful way. Instead, ask them what the best part of their day was and what the worst was. You'll hear some interesting stuff. And make sure that when they ask the same of you, you answer honestly.

———◦———

Buy a box of colored chalk and give your kids carte blanche to your sidewalk. It should provide hours of fun, and if the weather is right, they can hose it down for a grand finale.

———◦———

Kids love to play the game Memory. It involves placing cards face-down on a table and then turning them over to make pairs. If you order double photos, you can make your own memory game. It's much more meaningful, and young kids delight in matching their own, personal photos.

———◦———

Bake cookies. It costs very little to bake a big batch. They taste better than store-bought, and baking them is a great parent/child activity.

———◦———

Keep a scrapbook for your child that includes the front page of the newspaper on the day of his/her birthday every year. It's a great later-day gift.

———◦———

Examine snowflakes. Make a snowflake catcher and become a winter scientist. Make a square pocket from two 5-inch squares of black felt. Stitch three of the four sides closed. Make the felt square rigid by inserting a piece of plastic you've cut out from a plastic milk bottle. Then stitch the fourth side closed. Next, attach a piece of yarn to the square and tie a cheap plastic magnifying glass to the end of the yarn. Head outside with your kids when the white stuff begins to fall.

Water balloons are a great way for kids to have fun on a hot summer day. Fill them with a hose, tie the ends in a knot, and toss them. Make sure to keep the balloons away from very young children. Broken balloon pieces pose a choking threat.

Scrabble, Monopoly, Chess, Checkers, Parcheesi, and all those other games you used to play for hours when you were a kid are still every bit as much fun as they were then. They don't require electricity, there's no "mouse" to maneuver, and they provide a great way for a family to spend an evening together.

Grow a sunflower with your child. It's amazing to watch a tiny seed grow into a six-foot-high plant, and the seeds it produces are fun to roast.

Take out a tablecloth, cloth napkins, your good dishes, and a couple of candles and make dinner look special . . . for no reason at all.

Let your children roast marshmallows over a candle — with your close supervision, of course.

Pick up a cheap picture frame or recycle an old one to display your children's artistic endeavors. Hanging them on the wall will validate their efforts and give you years of pleasure as you look at them.

Talk to your oldest living relative about his/her childhood memories and record the conversation on tape. When this person is gone, feel good that you recorded the memories for safekeeping. While you're at it, try to pull together a family tree.

Edible Delights

If you have a craving for something (buttercrunch ice cream, ribs, olives, etc.) buy it, eat it, and enjoy it. If you spend a lot of time denying yourself because of calories, fat, or whatever, you'll end up eating twice as much of all kinds of other things . . . none of which will satisfy your craving.

———○———

One of my favorite simple pleasures is a perfectly baked potato topped with cheese, bacon, vegetables, or nothing at all. It's a great shortcut to bake a potato in the microwave. The truth is, however, that it tastes much better if you bake it slowly in the oven. We suggest a compromise. Give it a few minutes in the microwave and then finish it off in the oven.

———○———

Put a bunch of grapes in the freezer. They come out as hard as marbles and tasting like grape sorbet. Bite them, or let them melt in your mouth.

> *I adore simple pleasures. They are the last refuge of the complex.*
>
> **Oscar Wilde (1854–1900)**

Broil tomatoes for something different. Slice a tomato in half and sprinkle some sugar on the open, cut side. Place it under the broiler for a few moments. The sugar brings out the flavor and hastens the browning.

⊱──◦──⊰

What could be a more simple and satisfying pleasure than a large dish of creamy mashed potatoes that could be prepared ahead of time and heated up without losing its creaminess? For "mashies" that stay smooth, try this. Mash the potatoes with warm milk, butter, and an egg yolk. Whip an egg white and fold it into the potatoes. Place into a buttered casserole and dot with more butter. Cover and refrigerate until ready to use. Heat in a 400°F oven for half an hour before eating. Talk about comfort food!

⊱──◦──⊰

If you're looking for an easy way to fix a nutritionally sound breakfast, make a blender shake. Put vanilla or plain yogurt in a blender, add bananas or the fruit of your choice, drop in an ice cube or two, and puree. Presto! A delicious, quick meal that leaves you time to read the morning paper. Add brewer's yeast or protein powder for extra nutritional benefits.

⊱──◦──⊰

Pancakes are a simple pleasure in and of themselves; but if you've got children and a facility for whimsy, think about pouring a few snowman pancakes. Dinosaurs, flowers, hearts . . . it's all a matter of how much control you've got as you pour. Raisins make great eyes and buttons.

Melt some chocolate and dip in pretzels, strawberries, oranges . . . or fingers!

⊱—◦—⊰

Children really appreciate it when you make the effort to present them with special, attractive food. I had an aunt who always made me "pussycat-face" eggs. They were just flat omelets cut in the shape of a cat. I always make it a point, when I serve my son yogurt and fruit, to arrange the orange and apple slices like spokes, coming out of the yogurt cup in the center of the plate. It makes a difference. I actually have a ten-year-old who notices and says things like, "Nice plate," before he begins to stuff his face!

⊱—◦—⊰

If you live in an area where there's a long apple season, try drying your own apples. Simply core and peel your favorite varieties of apples and slice them . . . not too thin and not too thick. Lay them on a cake rack and place them in a 225°F oven for several hours. For a special treat, cut them up and mix them with nuts and raisins.

⊱—◦—⊰

Soup is usually not very expensive, even at a good restaurant. Buy a takeout bowl at your favorite restaurant and bring it home. It's a cozy treat for lunch, or add some bread and cheese and call it dinner.

Celebrating Life

In this chapter . . .

- *Making Traditions*
- *Breaking Traditions*
- *The Holiday Table*
- *Birthdays*
- *Other Family Celebrations*
- *Holiday Celebrations*
- *Preserving Memories*

H ow can we maintain the celebratory aspect of celebrations — birthdays, anniversaries, holidays — but keep the drudgery to a minimum? Earlier in this book I talked about how, after many years, my friend's "perfect" Christmas became an exhausting trial for her. While she was struggling with this issue she thought about abandoning Christmas entirely and perhaps going away for the holidays. She discovered, however, that there were less extreme alternatives. There are ways to celebrate Christmas, Passover, birthdays, Kwanzaa, and emerge from the celebration feeling renewed rather than depleted.

As in every chapter of this book, certain hints may contradict each other. The idea is to browse and come up with something that feels right to you. Keep in mind that if you try something and it doesn't work, give it up and try something else!

Making Traditions

Family traditions are magical for children. In my family, my mother and I polished the silver candlesticks every year before the Passover seder. I do it now with my two boys and they genuinely love doing it . . . because it's a holiday tradition. Another family I know makes popcorn balls every year for Christmas. It's sticky and messy and something they all look forward to doing. Yet another climbs a hill and flies kites every Easter Sunday. Your children may remind you of such customs — they often find great comfort and satisfaction in building traditions.

What works for someone else might not work for you. You might like to wait until the winter solstice to get your Christmas tree, whereas your neighbors bring theirs home the day after Thanksgiving. Some families like to dress up and go out for a special holiday dinner; others find that a huge drain of energy. Develop traditions that make your family feel relaxed and united.

Try creating your own celebrations — such as a "First Day of School Bus Stop Gathering." If your kids leave for school from a bus stop, try celebrating the first day of school with a brief party. Call the other parents who gather at the same stop and arrange for one person to bring drinks, another muffins, and another cups. Then meet fifteen minutes before the appointed time and toast your kids as they begin their new academic year.

The holidays are a great time to reach out to people who are less fortunate than you. It's also a good time for children to learn how much they can do and what a difference they can make. Try some of the following:

- Offer to drive a homebound person to visit family for Christmas.

- Read holiday stories to people with vision or literacy problems.

- Sing Christmas carols at a nursing home.

- Double up on your cooking and bring a meal to someone who wouldn't otherwise have it.

Kids love to hear about how you celebrated things when you were young. We live far away from most of my family, and my children like to hear about the big Chanukah parties we had when I was young, with all my aunts and uncles and cousins. Even better is hearing about how these holidays were celebrated by their grandparents . . . who might remember stories their parents told them about how things were done before they came to this country. All this gives a feeling of continuity.

Sometimes getting dressed up to celebrate a holiday adds to the feeling of festivity . . . even if it's just your immediate family celebrating in your own home.

⊱—◦—⊰

If you have children who find it a terrible chore to dress up for a holiday, try letting go of whatever image you've got in your mind and allowing everyone to dress as they please. Dirty jeans, pajamas . . . even if it feels kind of funky, it might be just what everyone needs to be in a festive mood.

⊱—◦—⊰

Times of celebration should also be times of reflection. It is a Jewish tradition to break a wine glass as part of a wedding ceremony as a remembrance of the destruction of the Temple. In other words, at our happiest moments we should take a moment to think about how difficult life can be. Ideally, this kind of reflection should not diminish your pleasure but, rather, enhance it.

> *I have often been downcast, but never in despair; I regard our hiding as a dangerous adventure, romantic and interesting at the same time. In my diary I treat all the privations as amusing. I have made up my mind now to lead a different life from other girls and, later on, different from ordinary housewives. My start has been so very full of interest, and that is the sole reason why I have to laugh at the humorous side of the most dangerous moments.*
>
> **Anne Frank (1929–1945)**

Make sure you allow for some downtime during a busy holiday season for your family to be alone … with each other.

Breaking Traditions

As wonderful as I just said holiday traditions are, make sure they don't become traps. Everyone involved should know that if they no longer find a tradition meaningful, it's up for discussion. For example, if your children are older and you're finding Thanksgiving less meaningful, get off the holiday circuit. Volunteer, as a family, to work in a soup kitchen. It's good to share the experience of sharing.

⊱━◦━◦━◦━⊰

Holidays can be wonderful times for families to gather. However, sometimes we all feel trapped by the obligation of family gatherings on the holidays. One year we were snowbound and couldn't make it up to Boston for our traditional family Thanksgiving. Lots of our friends in the small town in which we live were in a similar situation. We all got together and had a wonderful Thanksgiving … in which we gave thanks for our families and for the opportunity to have a celebration without them. No guilt, lots of fun, and the following year we had a much better time with our family!

⊱━◦━◦━◦━⊰

If you love to send cards for birthdays, anniversaries, and other occasions, by all means, do it. Make it easy on yourself, though, by buying greeting cards before you need them and by getting in the habit of looking for irresistible cards when you shop. I keep my greeting cards in a special box, and throughout the year I add to my collection. When I want to send a card, I always have one readily at hand.

⊱⊰

If you've hosted the traditional family Christmas, Chanukah, Easter, Passover for the last ten years, think about taking a year off and finding a place to be the guest!

⊱⊰

Take a day or two off before your holiday vacation so that you have enough time to enjoy preparations. Schedule that prep time into your holiday vacation time.

⊱⊰

Give yourself (and, if it works for you, your family) a mental health day . . . a "holiday" for no reason other than the fact that you deserve it. Think about making it a "family" holiday: everyone takes off from work or school, sleeps late, and goes to the beach, or skiing, or to an afternoon movie. I once called a friend who was in the midst of such a day and her nine-year-old answered the phone. "Why are you home?" I asked. He answered quite matter-of-factly, "Oh, I'm having a mental illness day." "No, no," I heard my friend shout in the background. "Not illness . . . health!"

⊱⊰

Share your holiday traditions with a family of a different religious background. Have them share their traditions with you.

The Holiday Table

As you approach a big holiday weekend, make sure you've got a full larder with all the things you'll need to ease the burden of unexpected company. For us, that means lots of tuna, pasta, pretzels, olives, nuts, eggs, cheese, and bread. With the right basics you can always throw together an easy dinner . . . especially if you don't create impossible culinary standards for yourself.

When you're doing the holiday cooking, give yourself a break by using a disposable roasting pan for your turkey/roast beef/ham. After your guests have left you'll be able to toss it in the trash and sit down to relax, rather than stand in front of the sink with a box of steel-wool soap pads and a lot of greasy water. It's not ecologically sound, though, so only indulge once a year.

Have you discovered clementines? Crates of these wonderful, seedless citrus fruits are usually abundant in greengrocers around Christmas time and make a fine, effortless dessert or gift.

Use pinecones for Thanksgiving or Christmas placecards. You can spray-paint the pinecone or leave it natural, and write the dinner guest's name on a small piece of white paper nestled between the scales.

Empty a jar or more of marinated artichoke hearts into a food processor for the world's easiest dip. Add to taste lemon juice, fresh garlic, and olive oil. Puree. Perfect for crusty bread or crudité.

⊱─◦─⊰

Kids love special-looking food. Try making birthday drinks a bit more special by freezing a cherry inside of each ice cube. You might want to do the same for the adults in your family. Cold white wine never looked better than it does with an ice-encased cherry floating in it.

Birthdays

A birthday is a time to focus on and celebrate a particular person. Don't rush around trying to create the perfect party; pay attention to the person instead. Whether it's a small child or a great-grandfather, express your love. Pamper them, listen to them, tune in to their feelings. And when it's your birthday, be just as nice to yourself!

⊱─◦─⊰

Every year, on the eve of my sons' birthdays, I tell them the story of the day they were born . . . leading up to the actual moment of birth. ("And all the doctors and nurses said, "Oh . . . he's just the most beautiful baby!") They never tire of hearing it, and we certainly never get tired of remembering those most miraculous moments!

Keep a scrapbook for your child that includes the front page of the newspaper on the day of his/her birthday every year. At some point he'll probably appreciate the history.

━┥◆◦◆┝━

We always allow the family member who's having a birthday to select the evening menu . . . within reason. It makes the day very special, and with a little bit of luck, there are leftovers to extend the feeling of the special day.

━┥◆◦◆┝━

Make a party for a friend on a special birthday. It's something they'll never forget.

━┥◆◦◆┝━

Don't bake a cake if it ends up being a chore. There are great mixes and, in a crunch, even bakeries! But if baking a cake is something that gives you pleasure, make it a point to find the time to do it — and enjoy it! Allow yourself to get carried away with the decorating. And take a picture of it when you're done.

━┥◆◦◆┝━

Any cake will look more special when it's decorated with curls of chocolate, and they're very easy to make. Simply scrape a chocolate bar with a vegetable peeler and enjoy the shavings.

━┥◆◦◆┝━

Drizzled chocolate is also a terrific cake-top decoration. The best way to melt chocolate is to break up a chocolate bar and put it in a plastic bag. Microwave it for a few moments, and then cut a very small hole in one corner of the bag. Squeeze the chocolate through as though you were holding a pastry bag.

How do you avoid a messy first piece of cake? Simply cut two slices right away, before you attempt to remove the first. The first will slide out without any problems.

It's a challenge to be both thoughtful in selecting gifts and also fairly efficient. Pick up gifts whenever you see something you think someone would like, rather than wait for the occasion. You'll have fewer last-minute hassles, as well as an ideal gift.

If you need a gift for a friend who has everything, make a contribution to an organization he/she is involved in or about which he/she feels enthusiastic. It's a double gift: first, it's money to a worthy cause; and second, it's less stuff for an over-stuffed friend to cope with.

Whenever you're in a large toystore or discount chain store, buy a few generic children's gifts and keep them on hand. You'll always have something ready for a birthday gift when you don't have time to shop.

Buy what you can from catalogs. It's fun to browse through them at your leisure, and you don't have to waste time going, looking, and buying.

Keep gift-wrapping paper, ribbons, a pair of scissors, and a roll of tape in a big box, so that whenever you go to wrap a gift you have what you need on hand.

⊳⊷⊶⊙⊷⊶⊲

Make wrapping a gift quick and easy. Loosely wrap your present in tissue paper and tuck it into a decorative paper bag (available at card stores). Drop the card inside, too. Your "package" looks festive but the time investment is nearly nil.

⊳⊷⊶⊙⊷⊶⊲

Let your children know that a gift need not be an object. They can make service coupons — for backrubs, breakfast in bed, vacuuming, and all kinds of other chores — that you can redeem whenever you want.

⊳⊷⊶⊙⊷⊶⊲

Don't over-invite when it comes to your kid's birthday party. Big parties can be overwhelming for young children. A good rule of thumb is to invite as many children as your child is years old ... plus one.

⊳⊷⊶⊙⊷⊶⊲

Turn your home into a movie theater for a child's birthday. Get the movies from your local library's film selection. For a special treat, have the birthday child design some tickets. And don't forget about a candy counter and the popcorn. While you're at it, make it a double feature.

⊳⊷⊶⊙⊷⊶⊲

If you've got a child with a winter birthday, suggest a beach party. All his friends can come with bathing suits, set up a big beach umbrella, fill sand buckets with goodies, and pass out inexpensive sunglasses. You won't have to worry about sun-block, but make sure the room is warm enough.

⊷⚬⚬⊶

Have a natural scavenger hunt for a child's birthday party. Let kids search for things like worms, pinecones, acorns, different-colored rocks, and flowers. It helps kids tune in to what's beautiful and marvelous in the world around them.

⊷⚬⚬⊶

If you have a child with a summer birthday, chances are lots of friends will be away . . . particularly as your child gets older. Think about celebrating the half-birthday with peers instead of the actual "big" day.

Other Family Celebrations

When a good friend or close relative has a baby, consider the following gift. Make a coupon redeemable for babysitting some time within the first few weeks. New parents are exhausted and usually quite nervous about using a "strange" babysitter. A trusted friend, on the other hand, is another story entirely and will offer them an opportunity to re-experience what it was like when it was just the two of them.

> *The aspects of things that are most important for us are hidden because of their simplicity and familiarity.*
> **Ludwig Wittgenstein (1889–1951)**

Weddings are the kind of events that often get out of hand. "Why am I doing this?" you may wonder as your mother starts booking fittings and meetings with florists and caterers. Well, it's a good question. Do it the way you want. You'll have a better time. After all, this is the start of your life with the family that you are creating.

⊱──⊰

Every few years it's a great idea to gather together with cousins, aunts, uncles, grand-aunts, grand-uncles, and all the second and third cousins once and twice removed. Just remember not to over-organize. Make sure there's plenty of time for relaxed talk and simple activities such as swimming and hiking, so that people can catch up with one another. Keep the more elaborate activities — visiting historic sites, museums, or amusement parks — to a minimum. Everyone will benefit from the fact that they have established or re-established friendships.

⊱──⊰

Although some families do very well with loose, unstructured time together, others appreciate the opportunity to learn something about where they come from, particularly from family elders. You can preserve these moments on video and either make copies for everyone or hold onto them as part of a family reference library.

⊱──⊰

If your extended family lives nearby, you can organize a fabulous meal for family gatherings by dividing up the courses and making pot-luck assignments. Let one generation bring the main course, another the salad, another the drinks, and another the bread. Or you can divide it up by family.

⊷—◦—◅⊶

Love means not having to spend a fortune on an anniversary gift.

Holiday Celebrations

For Valentine's Day, buy a pretty, small notebook; over the course of the year, make a note of the times your lover does something to remind you of why you got together in the first place. By the end of the year the notebook should make a nice gift. And if there's nothing in it, look around for someone else!

⊷—◦—◅⊶

You don't have to be Irish to celebrate St. Patrick's Day. We always enjoy it because, first of all, we love corned beef, cabbage, and Irish soda bread; and second, it takes place in March . . . a month with no other holidays, end of winter, middle of mud season . . . do you need more reason than that for a celebration?

⊷—◦—◅⊶

During the eight days of Passover, many families clean out their pantries of foods they are not permitted to eat. Sometimes they simply throw these foods out. More and more synagogues, however, have organized food pantry programs around this holiday. Call a synagogue near your home and see if you can bring your "chometz" (i.e., forbidden food) to them for transport to a nearby shelter.

For Labor Day, have an all-corn-on-the-cob dinner. Believe it or not, there are many ways of enjoying spectacular August corn. Mexicans use lime and pepper (it's great!). And you can make different flavored butters by whipping together some butter with jalepeño, with mint, or with basil or curry. It's healthy, it's cheap, and it's never better than at this time of year.

━┿━◆━◦━◈━┿━

Buy special pumpkin-carving knives for your kids at Halloween. These are available at most supermarkets in October, and they are absolutely safe. Then, let your kids do their pumpkins on their own.

━┿━◆━◦━◈━┿━

If your kids are too young to carve a pumpkin on their own, even with a safety knife, cut up lots of raw vegetables and lay them out with a tray of toothpicks. You can make a wild face with a carrot, broccoli, cauliflower, and spinach leaves! Add some markers to the tray in case anyone wants to draw.

━┿━◆━◦━◈━┿━

Try lighting more than one menorah during Chanukah. In fact, light one for each member of the family. Then, once they're lit, turn out the lights and watch the candles burn. It truly is a festival of light.

━┿━◆━◦━◈━┿━

One week before Christmas have a big family gathering, with all the aunts, uncles, cousins, and friends you can organize, and spend the day baking dozens of cookies. When you're all done, divide up the varieties and everyone will have an ample share of Christmas cookies.

Make a recording of your family caroling together every year. Children will love to listen to it year after year, and family that's far away will appreciate the recording as a gift.

***

If your Christmas tree lights are all tangled, plug in one plug so you can more easily distinguish one strand from another.

***

If you're concerned about safety because your active, curious toddler won't stay away from the Christmas tree, try putting some cement cinder blocks inside large boxes. Wrap the boxes so they look like gifts and arrange them at a safe distance from the base of your tree. Ideally, they'll be too big to climb on and too heavy to move.

***

If you've ever tried unsuccessfully to flambé a Christmas pudding, try heating the brandy before lighting it. (You can pour it into a large metal spoon and heat the spoon from underneath with a cigarette lighter or a candle.) Pour the warm brandy over the pudding, and it will be certain to flame when you touch it with a match.

***

Buy an amaryllis bulb for anywhere between $8 and $15. Follow the instructions that come with it, ask your local garden center for instructions, or see page 33 on how to force paperwhite narcissus, and you'll have an absolute show-stopper center-piece for the holiday table. If you have a green thumb, you may even be able to repeat this with the amaryllis bulb for successive years.

New York's Museum of Natural History has a Christmas tree that's decorated exclusively with origami. It's extraordinarily beautiful and most inspiring. Learn how to do it and give your tree a new look.

Decide one year to decorate your Christmas tree only with things found in nature: pinecones, bird nests, seashells, bittersweet, moss. It's free, and you'll be amazed how beautiful it is.

Don't wait for the holiday season to start buying Christmas presents. Do it all year long and put things away. In fact, the best time to buy a gift is right after Christmas ... when everything is marked down.

Preserving Memories

Photo albums — buy a new photo album every year with plastic sleeves for pictures. As the year goes by and you pick up your photos from the developer, open the album BEFORE you open the envelope of photos. Write the date and location of the photos on a piece of paper, slip it into the first sleeve of the album, and then select the best shots and put them in. Label the envelope with the date and location of whatever's left inside, and put it in the drawer that used to contain all those photos you plan to get to "someday."

As a rule, it makes sense to order a double set of photographs. The additional cost is nominal, and there's usually a grandparent, aunt, uncle, or friend who'd be happy to receive a great photo of your family.

Celebrations are usually great photo opportunities. Keep the following in mind:

- Keep your camera warm. Camera batteries lose energy in freezing temperatures. To be safe, stash spare batteries inside your coat pocket to keep them warm.

- Use natural illumination such as candles or a Yuletide blaze to add to the ambience of your photos.

- Low light levels require slow shutter speeds. If you get to a really slow speed, you'll need a tripod to avoid blurry photos.

- Avoid red-eye by making the room as bright as you can.

I have learned to have very modest goals for society and myself, things like clean air, green grass, children with bright eyes, not being pushed around, useful work that suits one's abilities, plain tasty food . . .

Paul Goodman (1911–1972)

Videos are the "moving" records of your family's life together. If you do the following, you'll have years of pleasure watching them.

- Check the power capacity of your batteries by watching a video on playback with a fully charged battery in the camera. If the battery isn't holding a full charge, it will shut down sooner than expected. It's best to know this before an important event rather than in the middle of it.

- If you've got a zoom, use it. This technique makes your video much more interesting to watch.

Check out the cost of having your parents' old home movies transferred to video tape. Your kids will get a kick out of watching your birthday party . . . and even if they don't, you will!

Do it, don't shoot it! Sometimes we become so obsessed with taking photographs and videos during celebrations that we miss out on the fun. Documenting a life is fine, as long as it doesn't interfere with living a life.

Less Is More

In this chapter . . .

- *Managing Time*
- *Managing Money*
- *Clutter Control*

A few years ago my parents became disabled and had to give up their home in Arizona, to move in with us in New York. The move was very difficult on many accounts, but it was complicated by the fact that there was so, so, so much in their home to be packed and moved. They weren't able to do the packing themselves, so we paid the movers to do it. When the truck pulled up our driveway there was an endless caravan of cartons, which we managed to unpack over the course of an entire year!

What was in the cartons? Well, three very large cartons were filled with empty jars, each one carefully wrapped in paper. There were mayonnaise jars, peanut butter jars, pickle jars, olive jars . . . virtually every kind of jar my mother had encountered in the fifteen years that she lived out west.

Another carton was filled with spice cans . . . again, each one carefully wrapped in paper. Many of the spices were decades old and had lost their aroma and taste. Other cans were nearly empty. A few were rusted shut. Also in those cartons were endless amounts of mail my parents had received over the years. Some of it was meaningful and special. Birth announcements dating back fifty years. A rent check from their first apartment. Wedding invitations. First drawings, report cards, and the like. Those special, meaningful notes made a pile that was perhaps two inches thick. The rest of the paper that had been packed and transported cross-country was, by any standards, meaningless. There were thank-you notes for dinner parties my mother had held . . . and she held them all the time. There were thank-you notes for gifts my parents had given to friends. There were magazines dating back thirty and forty years that weren't old enough to be of any value, but might one day be . . . had I not brought them all to the recycling center!

These cartons of "stuff" that we paid to have packed and wrapped, that traveled cross-country, and that we spent precious time unpacking and carting to the dump served as a valuable lesson. By the time the task was completed I vowed to go through my own home with a fine-toothed comb and get rid of everything I didn't really need. For all I know, my kids may one day be angry that I didn't save enough of their precious "stuff," but I'm convinced that the value is in the experiences we have much more than the mementos we stash away.

Clutter is time consuming . . . and it complicates our lives. The same issue of thinning out "stuff" applies to activities and (this will sound heartless) people. Our goal is to have a little breathing room, timewise. We'd all like more time to spend on more satisfying activities. In order to do this we must simplify — reduce the time spent on unrewarding activities or, where possible, eliminate them altogether. We will advise you to stop spending time with people that you don't like, and doing things simply because you didn't know how to say "no." If those hints feel comfortable to you, try them out. If they don't, move on. And as we economize on time, it's helpful to think about the "less is more" notion with regard to how we spend our money. Management of our time, our money, and our physical space — these are the three challenges we'll tackle in this chapter.

Managing Time

Make two master lists of all your responsibilities: at work and with your family. Write it all down, with the most important tasks at the top and the least important ones way down at the bottom. When you're finished (and make it as complete as you can), draw a line through the middle of the list and rarely, if ever, do any of the things beneath the line.

Simplicity, simplicity, simplicity! I say, let your affairs be as two or three, and not a hundred or a thousand; instead of a million count half a dozen, and keep your accounts on your thumb-nail.
Henry David Thoreau (1817–1862)

It's important to understand your own energy level over the course of a day. Are you a morning person or a night person? Do you hit an energy slump at the same time every day? There is no right or wrong way to be. It is wrong, however, to fight who you are. If you know that you're worthless in the morning, don't attempt to get a lot done then. Have a cup of coffee and read the paper. Save the work for the late hours, while others are asleep and you're hot to trot.

If you feel that you don't have time to complete things, break the job into smaller units. The garage needs organizing? Try attacking one wall at a time. No time to read a book? Maybe you do have fifteen minutes a day to read a few pages or a chapter . . . or better yet, try a short story.

Once you've determined exactly what is most important to accomplish in any given day, don't allow yourself to be interrupted until it is done. Don't take calls, don't break for coffee, and don't put in that load of wash. Do what you HAVE TO DO, and then get on to other things.

Making lists is a crucial way to organize your life and keep things simple. But always make a list you know you can accomplish. At the end of the day you'll feel good about what you've done rather than overwhelmed by what you haven't done. Failure is exhausting.

Keep a list of short calls you need to make, such as calls to arrange appointments, and make them early in the day. You can cross off several "to do" items from your list — a great way to start the day!

━━◦━◦━━

Sometimes it's easy to forget the calls you need to make because you get to the office and get caught up in the day. To remember, make a list of calls to be made the next day every night before you go to bed.

━━◦━◦━━

Every now and then you think of someone you haven't spoken to in a long a time and have an impulse to call . . . but it's too late, or you're about to walk into an important meeting. Write those names down when you think of them and you'll be more likely to get to them.

━━◦━◦━━

Learn to say "no" at work, as well as at home. Women have an especially hard time with this. Practice in front of a mirror. Someone asks, "Could you possibly stay late today and help me with my presentation?" "No," you say. "I'm sorry I can't help. I've really got to get home." Or, "Could you organize desserts for the school show?" "No, not this time," you say, "but perhaps another time."

━━◦━◦━━

Don't overschedule your children. Children (and adults, also, for that matter) need downtime . . . time to do absolutely nothing but lie on their backs in the grass and look up at the clouds. This kind of downtime is every bit as important as piano lessons, Little League, and gymnastics. Maybe even more so.

Junk the TV. If you can't bear to actually get rid of your tube, try putting it in a closet for a month. You'll be shocked by how much time you suddenly have. Read a book. Exercise. Do nothing. If you just can't bear to get rid of the TV, try using the VCR to protect against tel-oblivion. Record the shows you want to watch. This will force you to think about what it is you want to see and help keep you from watching just because the set is on. An added bonus of this regimen is that you get to fast-forward through commercials.

⊱───◦───⊰

Use your lunch time to regroup. If you've got an hour in the middle of the day for lunch, make the most of it. Perhaps you can find a quiet room to meditate in. On a sunny day sit outside and read, or take a long, vigorous walk. Meet a friend in a nice restaurant. You design the break to suit you, but keep in mind that the idea is to return to work feeling as if you've had some significant time off.

⊱───◦───⊰

Make use of your commute. Rather than thinking of commuting time as "lost" time, find a way to make the most of it. Some people who commute by car get hooked on books or great music on audio tapes or CDs. If you commute on public transportation, you can use a walkman to the same end. And if you live within walking distance of your workplace, think about doing the trip on foot. Bring along a pair of sneakers and you can decompress, exercise, and make your way home at the same time.

If you can afford it, hire help. Even if you can do everything yourself, there may be times when it makes more sense to shell out the cash and have someone else do the job. If, for example, you earn your living as a writer but are a capable carpenter as well, it may make more sense to hire someone to build bookshelves while you use the time to write an article . . . and sell it.

Try to arrive places a few minutes early. If you are habitually late, it may be because you are trying to cram in one last thing before you leave. Or you may fear that if you're early you'll waste time waiting for others. Make an effort to break the late habit — it adds stress to your life, causes you to drive too fast, and annoys the people waiting for you. Arriving early will give you a chance to take a deep breath, read a few pages, make a list, feel in control of your life.

It's a good idea to keep only one calendar or date book, and keep it with you at all times.

Try to plan some aspects of your days so that they are set and not open to negotiation. This kind of planning eliminates the energy involved in scheduling each day (or reinventing the wheel). Who makes breakfast, lunch, or dinner? You'll know the answer. Who's carpooling? It's all arranged. Now, do what you have to do and relax about the rest.

If mornings are wild and wacky at your house, try to have everything ready the night before:

- Get your family get into the habit of packing briefcases, school backpacks, and/or baby's diaper bag at night before bed. Stand these near the door.

- Have children pack their school lunches the night before and stick them in the fridge.

- Lay out your work clothing the night before — some people carry this even further and take the time on Sunday night to plan out their wardrobe for a week. You can always shift things around if you're just not in the mood for "Tuesday's dress," but at least you're assured a week's worth of clean, ironed, run-free, spot-free clothing.

- Keep pocket change in a bowl near the door so you have change when you need it . . . for calls from pay phones, school lunches, tolls for bridges, and the like.

- Keep a pad and pencil near the door for last-minute notes.

⊱⊶⊙⊷⊰

Set your alarm for a half-hour early every morning and think of that time as all yours. Lie in bed, listen to the radio, meditate, exercise, soak in the tub, or do whatever you need to do to prepare yourself for the day ahead.

⊱⊶⊙⊷⊰

Think about food preparation in terms of two kinds of time . . . "active" time and "total" time. "Active" time is the actual time it takes to prepare the meal: chop the onions, sauté, brown the meat, and so on. "Total" time is the time it takes from the moment you begin to prepare the meal until the meal is actually ready to eat. Before you think about preparing a meal, think about which kind of time you have available. A roast beef takes very little "active" time but quite a bit of "total" time. That makes it a great dinner party choice because you can sit and visit with your guests while the dinner is preparing itself. It's a lousy choice, however, if you come home late from work and need to eat quickly so the kids can get on with their homework.

Telephone calls are something we could all do with a lot less of . . . so set certain times of the day during which you simply don't answer the phone. Use that time to cook dinner in a peaceful, mindful way, or just to hang out with your family.

Consider getting rid of your answering machine. You'd avoid having to ever "return" a call.

Unless you work at home and positively cannot afford to ever miss a call, get rid of call-waiting. It's annoying to you and to the person you're speaking with. Anyone who really needs to reach you can wait until your line is no longer busy.

Even if your gas tank is only half empty, fill it while you're doing other errands. This will prevent an emergency stop or a special trip when the needle is dangerously below "E."

> *You must learn to be still in the midst of activity and to be vibrantly alive in repose.*
>
> **Indira Gandhi (1917–1984)**

Think about what you need to do on any given day and group your tasks so that you don't spend time retracing your steps. A friend once told me she put 100,000 miles on her car going nowhere . . . but going there over and over again.

If you have children, bring them along on errands when possible instead of arranging childcare. It is educational for them, and it can make a dull task interesting. Of course, some errands are fun with children in tow, but others are nearly impossible.

Check into automatic services that might save you a trip to the bank. You might, for example, have your mortgage payment automatically deducted from your checkbook.

Arrange carpools for your children's activities. Everyone benefits, including the environment.

Consider not making social plans for more than two weekends in a row. It's important to give yourself time every now and then on a weekend to have no plans. If you feel like pulling something together at the last minute, you can always do it.

⊱─◦─◦─◦─⊰

Think about the people you spend time with . . . on the phone or in person. How many of those relationships seem fulfilling? How many feel like habits? Think about your time as a valuable commodity, and don't waste it in company that isn't pleasing.

⊱─◦─◦─◦─⊰

Don't give up entertaining because it's too much work. Instead, make dinner parties potluck affairs. Everyone brings a course, and everyone goes home with one pot to wash.

⊱─◦─◦─◦─⊰

If you are married and both you and your spouse have full-time jobs, think about the possibility of one or both of you downshifting to part-time. To consider this you'll have to assess just how much money you actually need, and what it is you need the money for. Then, ask yourselves whether the things you are working for are as valuable as the time away from work might be. It's an issue many people never think about . . . but that's changing.

⊱─◦─◦─◦─⊰

When you get to work in the morning, use your first ten minutes to establish an overview of your day. In allocating time, allow open time to deal with unexpected events that you can't anticipate.

⊱─◦─◦─◦─⊰

Think about the meetings you have every week in your office, and list them in order of priority. See what it does to your productivity if you cut out the one on the bottom of the list.

If you have a second job, ask yourself why you have that job. If it's so that you can afford expensive and time-saving conveniences, chances are you might not need them if you weren't working!

><+>-0-<+><

Volunteering can be a great source of satisfaction. Before you volunteer, however, make sure that the work is something you are excited about and that there are people involved whom you really enjoy being with. If not, learn to say, "No."

><+>-0-<+><

Don't overcommit yourself. It's better to start out with a small commitment and build up than to start out overcommitted and have to decrease your involvement.

Managing Money

It's easy to get caught in a spiraling spending trap. We spend more and more money on things we really don't need . . . things that require maintenance and monthly expenditures. In the end, we find ourselves working to support a lifestyle that isn't all that important or satisfying. There is a growing movement of people who have decided to take control of the hundreds of dollars that dribble away every month. One of the gurus of that movement is Amy Dacyczyn, author of *The Tightwad Gazette*, a newsletter that for many years has published tips on how to save money. Many of the hints that follow are designed to get us back to what we need . . . and to put our money in the bank, where we will have it to pay for college, trips, and the things we consciously choose to spend it on.

Make a distinction between the things that you must have and the things that you simply desire. Before you buy something, always ask yourself if you *need* it or if you *want* it. If you don't need it, don't buy it. Instead, try putting the money that you might have used to buy it toward paying off your credit card balance. You'll be surprised by how big a dent you can make in your debt simply by doing that!

Study where your money goes. Do you really need cable? Is it worth $25 a month? What would you do with the time you spend in front of the TV if you didn't have it? How about those new shoes? Pay special attention to the monthly bills and add up everything you could comfortably do without. Then, experiment with making cuts. Keep in mind that you can always put things back into your budget that you've cut out.

Live below your means — if you come into a windfall, don't spend it all. Put most of it away (after a slight indulgence) and live as you always did. At some point you'll find the right place for that money!

Use a charge card that must be paid in its entirety every month. That way, you won't spend money you don't have.

If you lay out money for a business expense by charging it to your own credit cards, keep your reimbursement check until your credit card bill arrives. If you cash the checks when you get them, you might spend the money and find yourself short at the end of the month when the bills come in.

———○———

Don't renew a subscription to a magazine that you don't really have time to read. If you subscribe to a magazine that you love and read every month, by all means continue subscribing; but keep in mind that most of us get ample opportunity to read magazines while we're waiting for doctors, dentists, hair stylists, and so on.

———○———

Never assume that someone is giving you the lowest price on anything just because they tell you they are. Shop around. You can even do it by phone or the internet.

———○———

If you see something on sale that you need (such as your child's favorite brand of sweat pants), buy more than one. It's true that we're advocating "less is more," but "more" at a cheaper price is "less" in the long run.

———○———

You can save a good deal of money by setting up a babysitting co-op. The up side is that you can develop a set of chits as a substitute for cold cash. The down side, of course, is that you have to spend time caring for other people's kids as often as they care for yours. For many new parents, however, free time away is well worth the sacrifice.

Try to use cash. If you're going out to dinner, stop at an ATM (automatic teller machine — preferably one that doesn't charge a fee) and get the cash you need to pay. If you're going shopping, do the same. Long after you've digested your food and worn your new clothing, you won't have any bills to anticipate.

If you get into the habit of eating what's in season, you'll pay considerably less for vegetables and probably be eating a healthier diet as well. Eating only what is in season is one of the tenets of a macrobiotic diet.

You'll be amazed at how much money you can save by bringing your lunch to work at least three times a week.

Convenience foods cost more and aren't always that convenient. A frozen lasagna, for example, costs much more than one you make yourself; and if you double the recipe when you make yours from scratch, you'll have some homemade convenience food right in your freezer.

Think about giving up meat. It's costly and really quite unnecessary. If you're not ready to give it up entirely, think about cutting back on it substantially.

Americans eat way too much food. You might even consider fasting every now and then. Check with your doctor before you fast, however, to make sure you're in good shape for it.

Everyone knows how much you can save by clipping coupons. The problem is that many of us clip them but don't have them with us when we need to use them. Avoid this problem by keeping your coupon folder in the car. That way it's always there when you pull up to the store for a last-minute item.

Get together with a group of friends and form a spice-buying collective. When you buy spices in bulk they're fresher and much, much cheaper.

Join a food co-op. Your unit cost may be less than the retail price, and you'll consume healthier foods and more "green" household products.

Switch over to rechargeable batteries.

You can save a fortune on games and toys for your kids if your community has a toy library. Like book libraries, toy libraries are places from which you can borrow all kinds of toys. To find out where the nearest one is, send a self-addressed stamped envelope to the USA Toy Library Association, 2530 Crawford Avenue, Suite 111, Evanston, Illinois 60201.

Instead of paying a fortune for fancy children's bandages, keep some stickers on hand so your kids can decorate their bargain-priced ones.

If you live in or are going to visit a city, buy a roll of tokens to be used on the bus or subway. You'll have a great deal more freedom of movement if you don't have to piece together the "right" change.

If you're in a city, it's important to have a roll of quarters for pay phones. (In some places a phone call still costs a dime.)

Having a computer and getting on line may seem a bit out of synch with the idea of "less-is-more." E-mail, however, is a great way to cut down on your long-distance phone bill and communicate with friends and family who live a long way off. So, if you're set up with everything you need, before you pick up the phone to make a call, E-mail instead.

Think twice before buying a new car. Yes, they're shiny and clean, but hefty monthly car payments are burdensome. If you must buy one, buy last year's model as soon as the new year's model comes out. Better yet, buy last year's demo. You stand a chance of a getting a deal!

Automobile dealers usually pay their sales staff a commission based on the amount of gross profit the salesperson develops from the sale of a vehicle. In addition to this regular commission, monthly volume bonuses are usually paid when a certain number of units have been sold. The later part of the month is when the sales staff is most eager to get the units they need to reach their goal so they can collect these substantial bonuses. This includes sales managers and assistants. You could reap a considerable savings if you make it a point to negotiate a new car sale late in the month.

If you plan to trade in your car as part of the negotiation on a new car, you owe it to yourself to get the best possible price for it. Blue books only offer estimates. The way to gain a sense of the value of your trade-in is to shop around. Go to several used car dealers and see what kind of offers you get. Armed with that information, you can negotiate a price that's fair to you.

One of the hidden expenses of shopping by mail is handling and postage charges. You can reduce this expense by pooling your orders with friends and splitting the cost.

Think about what your talents are and what your needs are, and try to get things done without having any money exchange hands. If your kitchen needs painting, for example, and you know a painter who has just had a baby, offer him the crib your kids have outgrown. This kind of offer will accomplish two things: first, you'll get yourself a free paint job, and second, you'll get rid of the crib that is cluttering up your spare bedroom or basement.

Forget about first-run movies. Before you know it, the movies everyone is standing in line to see (and paying $7 for) will be playing at discount theaters. And in another few months you'll be able to rent them for the entire family to watch for only $2.

If you love children's books, as I do, but don't want to spend money for the very expensive hardcover editions, buy them in paperback and apply clear contact paper to the front and back covers — both inside and out. My oldest son is sixteen years old, and we still have his contact-paper–covered childhood copy of *Caps For Sale* . . . in perfect condition.

Don't go shopping as a form of entertainment; you'll end up buying things you don't really need. If you're bored or want to treat yourself, try the following instead of spending money: go for a walk; check out a book, CD, or movie from the library; call a friend or family member to whom you haven't spoken in a long time; or go out for coffee or tea in an unfamiliar café.

Limit your wardrobe to three colors that go well together. You will always have something that matches something else, and old clothing will blend well with newer clothing. If you fall in love with something that's different from your usual colors, make it a jacket or sweater; but stick with the basic colors for skirts, pants, and shirts. (The friend who offered this tip is quick to add that you can never go wrong with purple!)

Share dress-up clothing. If you have a few friends who are fairly close in size, get together on a "formal" outfit. These are the gowns, tuxedos, and dress shoes that you wear once every few years but that cost a fortune. This advice is also valuable for children. Hang on to those dress-up shoes, dresses, and blazers and share them. Save your money for a good winter coat that you'll wear every day for five months of the year!

Given the choice between buying a few cheap things or one high-quality item, buy the single treasure. You'll feel very special when you put it on.

Buy fewer pairs of shoes but make sure they are good ones. Better shoes can be repaired; consequently they have a longer life and save you money. Cheap shoes are like disposable plates. Use them and toss them.

Buy clothes that fit. Some people think they save money by buying their children clothing that's way too big. The idea is that they'll grow into it eventually and will get extra seasons out of it. Keep in mind that when you do this the clothing never really looks the way it should. At first it looks too big, and by the time it fits it's worn out.

If your daughters dress in tights, you know how expensive that can be. You can save a considerable amount of money by turning a pair of tights that's full of pulls inside out. They'll look like new.

To save money on children's clothing, focus on hand-me-downs and thrift shops . . . especially shops that specialize in kids' clothing. However, never accept hand-me-downs unless you know you're going to use them. Otherwise, you're just assisting someone who wants to clean out her closets by filling up yours!

Clutter Control

The best way to clear your life of clutter is to make believe you're moving and go through your house room by room — pruning ruthlessly.

Take your clutter temperature. Be honest with yourself about your own personal tolerance for clutter. Clutter can make your life more difficult, but each of us has a different tolerance for it. Some people actually feel anchored by a certain degree of clutter; if you're one of those people, you need to create the kind of life that will make you comfortable. Minimalism might make one person's life easier but give someone else an anxiety attack.

Guard against stacks. Sort things out as soon as they come into your home, or the moment you are finished with them. Whenever you put something into a pile "to be sorted out later," it simply doesn't get done.

If you pick up your mail at the post office, get rid of the junk before you come home. Don't allow those sale flyers and tacky catalogs into your home. When you do this you save on two fronts: first, you avoid a build-up of clutter; and second, you don't have to pay for disposal.

Find a place to put your mail every day and never deviate from it.

As a rule, we recommend having less of everything. Wastebaskets, however, are a thing you simply can't have enough of. If you've got one in every room, you'll be much more likely to get rid of stuff.

Children's outgrown clothing should be put away promptly until it's suitable for younger siblings, or packed and given to someone who can use it. This requires sorting through drawers and closets at the end of each season and really thinning. No one child, for example, needs thirty T-shirts. Pick out his or her twelve favorites and get rid of the rest.

Make it a rule to never leave a room without picking up something that needs to be put elsewhere . . . and put it where it belongs.

> *The art of being wise is the art of knowing what to overlook.*
>
> **William James (1842–1910)**

Go through your pantry and refrigerator and put all the food you never use but have somehow acquired (anchovies, sardines, oatmeal, cardamom, whatever) in a large bag. Give the bag to a friend/shelter/church, or take it to the dump.

⊳┼◆○◆┼◁

If, as you go through your pantry getting rid of food you never use, you recall precisely why you bought it, use it. Make that anchovy chicken breast dish you read about when you went out and bought those anchovies . . . and enjoy it. Then, don't buy another tin of anchovies until you're ready to use them.

⊳┼◆○◆┼◁

Remove duplicate gadgets. You don't need three vegetable peelers and five strainers. The truth is you only need one of each. One soufflé dish (if you tend to make soufflés), one pan in each size, and not nearly all the Tupperware that's jammed into your cabinets. When you've accumulated all your duplicates, join with some friends for a multi-family tag sale.

⊳┼◆○◆┼◁

Health and beauty products often lose effectiveness over time. In addition to clearing out your medicine chest regularly, go through makeup, hair products, and lotions that you don't use and toss them.

Linen closets tend to accumulate family relics — your good sheets, your torn-up old sheets, your mother's old sheets, your mother-in-law's old sheets. Count the beds in your house and hold on to two sets of linen for each bed. Use what you need of the rest to make rags, and get rid of whatever is left over.

Go through your personal phone book and cross out the names of people whom you no longer call. If you ever need to reach them, you'll find a way; in the meantime, your personal phone book will be much less cluttered.

Make your own cookbook. This requires a bit of time outlay, but it's worth it. Buy a ring-binder style photo album with plastic-coated pages in which you lift the plastic to insert your photos. Take all the recipes you've clipped from newspapers and magazines over the years and place them in the album, with section dividers to make its use easier. As no one knows better than you do, many of your best recipes are those loose ones. Now you won't have to search for them, and they'll be protected.

Whenever you get a catalog that does not interest you, call the company immediately and request to be taken off their mailing list. Do likewise when you get duplicates.

If you haven't ordered something from a catalog in two months, put it into your recycling bin.

How often do you actually go back and read an old magazine? Rather than save stacks of them, clip any articles or recipes that you think you'll want to reference in the future and put them in a file. Then, get rid of the magazine. A good rule of thumb is to dispose of any magazine that's more than two months old.

Develop a tradition with your kids. Every year before their birthday and again before Christmas or Chanukah, have your children go through their toys and games and make a pile of what they're ready to give away. Remind them that they need to clear away old things to make room for new things. Bring all their old toys that are still in good shape to a shelter . . . and let your kids know what you're doing with them. It will make everyone feel good.

Any clothing that you haven't worn for two seasons should go either into the trash, to Goodwill, to a friend, or to the local thrift shop. Don't save things with the idea that you will eventually lose weight and fit into them again. It's just a way to punish yourself!

Throw away anything you have been unable to use because it's broken and you need to get it fixed (but haven't), or it's missing a part that "I'll have to find" (but haven't). All that stuff is taking up space.

Single earrings? Gather them all together and give them to your son!

Alphabetize your CD collection. This may seem a bit compulsive, but it makes it much easier to get your hands on what you want when you want it. And the less time you spend searching for what you want to hear, the more time you have to hear it.

⊳⊶⊙⊷⊲

When you take books out of the library, make a note on your calendar for the day before they're due. That way you're not likely to miss it.

⊳⊶⊙⊷⊲

If you have athletes in your house — or if you are one — spend the money for one of those sports racks you see advertised in catalogs, or reproduce one yourself. There should be room for every kind of ball (soccer, tennis, football, basketball, lacrosse, etc.) as well as bats, rackets, golf clubs, and everything else that might otherwise be left on your lawn or in the back of your car.

⊳⊶⊙⊷⊲

These days, most of us renew our driver's license in the mail. Make certain that you turn it around the same day you get it. It's not one of those things you can afford to lose in a pile.

⊳⊶⊙⊷⊲

Opposed to war toys? Send any old war toys you might have accumulated in your household to the National Coalition on Television Violence, P.O. Box 2157, Champaign, IL. 61820. This group hopes to hammer, melt and bend these toys of violence into a sculpture for peace. Explain this to your kids.

Close the door. You have a right to simply close the door and forget about whatever kind of mess is behind it. Everyone has a messy closet, or drawer or . . . yes . . . even a messy room. If the rest of your house is pretty much in order, give yourself a break and be grateful for the fact that wood is not transparent.

Organizing for Simplicity

In this chapter . . .

- *Kitchen Hints*
- *Quick Tips for Food*
- *Meal Planning and Food Shopping*
- *Organizing Your House*
- *Housecleaning*
- *Laundry*
- *Home Maintenance and Repair*
- *Safety*
- *Cars*
- *Family Living*
- *Travel*

T here are all kinds of things we do that complicate our lives. Until now, we've talked primarily about simplifying in an effort to find a general sense of satisfaction. We've talked about simplicity as the Shakers might have defined it . . . a simple life . . . a life uncomplicated by meaningless clutter.

There is, however, a practical aspect to simplicity as well. Anything we can do to shave moments from the tasks that eat away at our time is worth considering. The more efficient we are, the more time we have for what we care about, and the more time we preserve for the people and activities we value, the more satisfied we will feel. How does it simplify our lives if we learn the best way to clean a window? Well, if window-cleaning takes one hour rather than two, we might have an extra hour to sit with a child and read . . . or to lie in a hammock and listen to Louis Armstrong and Ella Fitzgerald make beautiful music together.

Kitchen Hints

Keep a good, large pair of scissors right next to your stove. You can snip fresh herbs into whatever you're cooking and avoid messing up a cutting board. You can also use the scissors to cut chicken cutlets, fish fillets, and much more.

▷─◁▷─◦─◁▷─◁

If you do the following when you load and run your dishwasher, dishes will wash more efficiently and come out cleaner:

- Make sure the hot water temperature is between 120° and 140° Fahrenheit.
- Keep silverware from nesting by loading some handles up and some down.
- Add a rinse aid to make water molecules wetter and dishes dryer.
- Load glasses in the rows provided, not over the tines of the rack.

If you drop an egg on the floor, sprinkle the mess heavily with coarse salt and leave it alone for five or ten minutes. The dried egg is easily swept into a dustpan.

It's easier to handle hot cupcake/muffin tins if you leave one of the corners empty. Equipped with an oven mitt and the empty cup as a grab bar, you won't have any trouble lifting the tin in and out of the oven.

If you don't have a fridge with a crushed ice dispenser, try making crushed ice this way. Fill a large freezer bag with cold water and close it tightly. Lay the bag on a baking sheet so that the water spreads out in it, and put the entire thing in the freezer. When you need crushed ice, take the bag out of the freezer and drop it on the floor a few times.

When you finish a box of tissues, put the empty box on a kitchen counter and stuff it with flimsy plastic grocery bags. Once you have a full box of bags, keep it in the trunk of your car. You'll be surprised how often those bags come in handy as a place to put muddy boots, dirty rags, plant seedlings, and more.

Think about your cooking style while you're working in the kitchen and equip your kitchen accordingly. Hang measuring spoons, wooden spoons, oven mitts, and the like where they are most readily accessible. Always keep your most frequently used cooking tools within easy reach.

Line a wall in your kitchen with cork so you have a place to tack up "must-have" items . . . such as permission slips, bills to pay, notes to answer, and so on.

$\rightarrow\!\!\leftrightarrow\!\!\bullet\!\!\leftrightarrow\!\!\leftarrow$

If you've got little kids, make sure they can reach the things they need. If the juice is on the top shelf of the fridge, don't expect anything other than, "Can I have a drink?" If it's where they can reach it themselves, they're more likely to do it.

$\rightarrow\!\!\leftrightarrow\!\!\bullet\!\!\leftrightarrow\!\!\leftarrow$

Don't bother to actually wash the grills on your barbecue. Just burn it all off and scrape it down with a wire brush.

$\rightarrow\!\!\leftrightarrow\!\!\bullet\!\!\leftrightarrow\!\!\leftarrow$

You can avoid lots of spattering when you fry meat if you sprinkle a bit of salt into the pan before adding the fat.

$\rightarrow\!\!\leftrightarrow\!\!\bullet\!\!\leftrightarrow\!\!\leftarrow$

The best oil to use on a butcher-block counter is mineral oil. Any cooking oil will do, but mineral oil will never go rancid.

$\rightarrow\!\!\leftrightarrow\!\!\bullet\!\!\leftrightarrow\!\!\leftarrow$

The worst part of broiling is cleaning the pan. It becomes a breeze, however, if you lay a paper towel over it, squirt dishwashing liquid on the paper towel, and then soak the paper towel with hot water. By the time you're finished eating, the broiler pan will be easy to clean.

Fill the sink with warm sudsy water when you're entertaining and put all flatware and dishes in the water until your guests leave. It makes for an easy cleanup.

⊱──◦──⊰

Every now and then, put your dish drainer into the dishwasher to get it really clean.

⊱──◦──⊰

Clean a standard oven without scrubbing by placing a small bowl of ammonia inside it, closing the door, and leaving it there overnight. Next day, wipe the inside of the oven with a rag. (Not recommended for self-cleaning ovens.)

⊱──◦──⊰

The best way to get wax off silver candlesticks is to pop them in the freezer for an hour or so. When you take them out, the wax will peel off easily without injury to the silver.

⊱──◦──⊰

Rather than spend your time scrubbing to renew a shine, bring the shine back to your aluminum pans by boiling water in them that has been mixed with a teaspoon of cream of tartar. They'll look like new with absolutely no elbow grease.

⊱──◦──⊰

The most energy-efficient units have the freezer on top. When the freezer is on the bottom, it's close to the heat-producing motor and more energy is required to keep things cold. That means higher electric bills and less money for the things you really care about.

Your fridge and freezer are most efficient if you keep them two-thirds full, if the freezer temperature is 0°F, and if the refrigerator temperature is 37°F.

⊱──◦─◦─◦──⊰

If you can trace a nasty kitchen odor to your garbage disposal, try tossing in a lemon and some oranges. The ground-up citrus eradicates the bad smell.

⊱──◦─◦─◦──⊰

Ant repellent — squeeze the juice of a lemon on ant paths. Ants will also retreat from lines of talcum powder, chalk, or cayenne pepper. Or combine equal parts of Borax and confectioners sugar and put the mixture in a flat dish under the sink or wherever you see the creepy-crawlers. They won't be there the next day.

⊱──◦─◦─◦──⊰

Rather than scrubbing the grease-caked metal filter above your stove, place it in the dishwasher and the work is done for you.

There should be less talk; a preaching point is not a meeting point. What do you do then? Take a broom and clean someone's house. That says enough.

Mother Teresa (1910–)

Quick Tips for Food

Buy a large, flat Tupperware container for salad greens and wash a week's worth every Sunday night. Not having to wash salad all week long is a great treat, and it opens up the opportunity for lots of easy dinners. For example, just add feta and olives and you've got a Greek salad.

━━◦◦◦━━

Chop a few onions in a food processor and put them in a plastic bag in your freezer. Most good meals begin with sautéing chopped onions, and this kind of preparation makes it easy. While you're at it, you can do the same with garlic, peppers, and anything else you use regularly.

━━◦◦◦━━

A simple way to melt chocolate is to break it up and pour boiling water right on top of it. In less than a minute you can pour off the water and the chocolate will be soft enough to add to your other ingredients. It won't melt into the water.

━━◦◦◦━━

The best way to marinate meat is to place it in a large plastic bag and put the bag in a deep bowl. Pour the marinade into the bag with the meat, close the bag tightly, and allow it to stand at room temperature for two or three hours. An alternative is to leave it overnight in the refrigerator. Every now and then, press the bag against the meat in several places to distribute the liquid evenly.

Try to keep a bag of frozen peas on hand. You can use it as a cold pack for minor injuries.

If you're waiting for bread dough to rise, bring a kettle of water to a boil on top of the stove. Place the bowl of dough inside your cold oven with the hot kettle. If necessary, reheat the kettle and replace it from time to time.

Ever wonder what to do with wilted, dressed salad? The English suggest adding a couple of chopped onions, some fresh (or frozen) peas, and boiling it all in 1½ pints of chicken broth. Once it's boiled for about five minutes, pour the whole thing into your food processor. They call it Sad Salad Soup.

If there's fat on the surface of your cooled soup, drop five ice cubes into it and the solidified fat will adhere to the cubes. Pick them up quickly with a slotted spoon.

If you have a stew or pot roast recipe that calls for "browning" meat, put the meat on a rack in a shallow pan and broil on high until the top is browned. Turn it and brown the other side the same way. The fat will drip to the bottom and you'll be ready to proceed with your recipe.

Carrots and many other vegetables can be cleaned with a small steel or natural bristle brush, rather than peeled.

When you make soup with onions and carrots, don't bother to peel them. Just rinse them well. The skin adds a nice color and lots of good vitamins to the broth.

When demolding Jello and mousse, forget about using hot water. The best way to demold these creations is to turn them upside-down on a platter and blow with your hairdryer. Just a quick turn of hot air and the mold lifts easily.

Cheese won't stick to your grater if the grater is sufficiently cold. Try holding it under cold water, or popping it in the freezer for a few minutes, before you begin using it.

If you need soft butter but yours is hard as a rock, try grating it. Put a bit of flour on the grater to prevent the butter from sticking.

Grate orange and lemon rinds and put into small, teaspoon-sized packets in your freezer. They'll be ready when you need them for flavoring or baking.

If you want to make dried herbs taste fresh, chop up an equal amount of parsley and add it to the herbs. The moisture and chlorophyll are a magical combination.

Keep some powdered buttermilk on your pantry shelf to use in a pinch.

Refresh withered parsley by putting it in a bowl of hot water and letting it stand for a few minutes. Shake it and put it in the fridge.

———o———

Parsley will stay fresh for up to two weeks if you trim the bottom of the sprigs (just as you would with fresh-cut flowers) and place them in a glass of water in the fridge.

———o———

All kinds of nuts freeze very well. If you don't keep nuts in the freezer, make sure they are stored in a cool, dry place. The refrigerator is great.

———o———

You can freeze bricks of cheddar, mozzarella, Gouda, Muenster, Swiss, and Camembert cheese without sacrificing flavor or texture. Cut them into ½-pound pieces, not more than one inch thick, and wrap them carefully. Thaw them with the wrapper on, in the refrigerator.

Meal Planning and Food Shopping

If you're lucky enough to work in an office with an employees' fridge, pack a week's worth of food for lunch and bring it in on Monday. Packing five yogurts, a loaf of bread, muffins, sliced turkey breast, and a six-pack of soda or juice once a week is simpler than spreading mayo every morning while everyone else in your household is making demands on you!

If peanut butter and jelly sandwiches are your kids' staple, here's how to keep them from getting soggy: Spread a thin layer of peanut butter on both pieces of bread. It acts as a barrier to keep the jelly from soaking through.

When you go to the trouble of making pancakes and waffles, make a few extra and freeze them in a zip-lock bag. Next time you want one, just pop it in the toaster. It's cheaper than buying the frozen varieties.

Develop a base list of what you need to have on hand for your family. Salt, flour, rice, bread, peanut butter, jam, chicken breasts, chicken broth, Cheerios . . . you know how you eat and what most often requires replacement, but having the basics written down is a way to avoid ever running out.

Take the family shopping with you and give each person a part of the shopping list. Splitting up the job will cut down your time considerably.

Keep your shopping list on your fridge door and let everyone note down what's missing as they eat your cupboards bare. If you always shop in the same place, organize the list by aisles. Bring a family member with you, tear the list in half, and attack it with two separate carts. It will be done before you know it.

Try to avoid shopping for dinner on your way home from work. It may seem like an efficient way to operate, but by the time you get home you will feel that much more tired, and cooking dinner will become a more exhausting task. Instead, conserve your energy and make do with whatever you find in your pantry.

Make sure your refrigerator has things in it that everyone wants so you don't have to think too much about mealtime. If you're serving meatloaf and one of your children hates it, he can always have a yogurt.

Develop a repertoire of at least five meals that you can prepare in less than thirty minutes.

One-dish meals, such as hearty soups, stews, and curries, are great time savers ... both on the preparation and the cleanup end of things.

To assess how much time a recipe will take, look at the following:

• How many ingredients are required?

• Is any pre-cooking of ingredients required (par-boiling, browning, etc.)?

• How much chopping and slicing is required?

• How many of the recipe steps require measuring?

• How many pots and pans are required to pre-pare the entire dish?

Before you attack a recipe, lay out everything you'll need on the counter. Include little bowls for all the pre-measured ingredients. If you chop and pre-measure your ingredients, the actual time you spend cooking will be very short.

When both parents work outside the home, family dinners can be difficult to choreograph. Often, they're rather late. You can protect the family mealtime gathering by preparing a snack plate for your kids every evening at around five o'clock. (If you aren't home from work by five, prepare it the night before and leave it in the fridge.) It can include all kinds of bite-sized leftovers from the night before (meat, cheese, pizza, etc.) along with leftover veggies and some fresh raw vegetables and fruit as well. If you know that your kids have had a healthy snack, you'll feel more relaxed about getting food on the table. If they eat . . . great. If they don't "finish their supper," you won't have to worry. Everyone can relax and enjoy each other's company, instead of worrying about who's eating what.

Avoid planning a meal in which everything requires elaborate preparation. If you're planning an elaborate salad, stick with a simple main course. If the main course requires lots of attention, keep the vegetable simple. Baked potatoes are always great!

Never confuse movement with action.
Ernest Hemingway (1899–1961)

Prepared, convenience foods are expensive and generally not as healthy as foods you make from scratch. Having said that, we must add that they have their place. Keep a prepared frozen lasagna, pizza, TV dinner, pot pie, or some other variation on that theme in your freezer. There are times when convenience is more important than anything else!

━┼◆━◦━◆┼━

Decide on eight or ten basic meals that you like and always keep the ingredients for them on hand.

━┼◆━◦━◆┼━

When you're really feeling in the mood to cook, double all recipes and freeze the extras. Cooking double quantities rarely takes much extra effort or time. Stews and casseroles are especially well suited to this. Then, if you feel like having friends over or just taking a night off, you've got dinner in the freezer, ready to go.

━┼◆━◦━◆┼━

If you double the quantities when you prepare meals with the intention of freezing the extras, remember one option is to freeze them in small, individual-portion containers. It's easier to defrost and much more useful.

━┼◆━◦━◆┼━

If you've got lots of little bits of leftovers in the refrigerator, turn dinner into a diner. Make up a menu, including drinks, and let your children put in their order. If two people order the same thing, tell them you've just sold out. It's fun and a great way to clear out leftovers without any waste.

Consider rice and pasta salads when you think of leftovers. Leftover chicken — mix it with some chopped-up celery, seasoning, salad dressing, and either rice or pasta. The same goes for leftover meat or fish. Add some tomatoes and basil if they are in season and toss it all together.

Organizing Your House

Pegboard (also called "clutter cutter") can be useful in lots of places other than a workshop. It's a great way to organize a child's room, an office, or a pantry.

⊱─◦─◦─⊰

Those tiny, powerful hand vacuums are enormously useful. It's a good idea to have one on each level of your house: one near the bedrooms, one in the kitchen, and another in the workshop. Cleaning up a mess becomes a "nothing-to-it" task and is less likely to be left undone.

⊱─◦─◦─⊰

Screw a hook onto your kitchen wall in an unobtrusive place and get into the habit of hanging your car and house keys on it as soon as you come into the house. This is especially helpful when there is more than one driver in the family.

⊱─◦─◦─⊰

If each member of your family has a basket for mittens, gloves, hats, and scarves near the door most frequently used, and puts them in when entering the house, you'll always know where they are.

We all know we should have a pad and pencil near the phone. Of course, knowing what we need and doing what we need are two separate things. To ensure that you've got what you need when you need it, buy an erasable memo board and nail it to the wall near the phone. Most of them come with pens that are attached by string. Perfect!

━━◆━◇━◈━◇━◆━━

Create a stationery drawer containing paper, envelopes, address book, pens, and a book of stamps. When you have a moment, glue the stamps onto the envelopes. It's one thing to write a letter and quite another to actually mail it. If the envelopes are already stamped, you'll never have to go searching.

━━◆━◇━◈━◇━◆━━

Keep a duplicate of your address book in a safe, fireproof box. Think about what it would mean to you if it were lost!

━━◆━◇━◈━◇━◆━━

Create your own library and clip from the newspaper items you think are worth saving. You might want to make files for Travel, Gardening, Cooking, Money, and so on. You'll be amazed at how often you use these.

━━◆━◇━◈━◇━◆━━

Buy several pairs of scissors and rolls of tape and sprinkle them around the house: one in each bedroom, two in the den or playroom, several in the kitchen. Do the same for pencils and pens. The time you save searching for those items will make the small expense well worth it.

Don't restrict your roll of paper towels to a kitchen setting. Keep a roll in the trunk of your car, and consider hanging a holder in the bathroom . . . especially if your kids run dirty hands under the faucet and then wipe off the dirt on your nice terry towels.

⊱────◦────⊰

Buy at least two dozen washcloths, preferably when they're on sale. You can dispense with those little hand towels entirely. Washcloths are inexpensive, big enough to dry your hands on, and great for all kinds of spills and small cleaning jobs as well.

⊱────◦────⊰

Always keep an extra roll of toilet paper in plain view. There's nothing more frustrating when you're in someone else's house than running out and not knowing where to look.

⊱────◦────⊰

If yours is a one-bathroom household, think about installing a second sink. It will enable two people to brush their teeth, comb their hair, or wash up at the same time.

⊱────◦────⊰

If you spend any time at all looking for your eyeglasses, get one of those eyeglass strings and wear it around your neck. Don't be embarrassed about it. You'll "see" the value of this tip within hours of the time you start using it.

⊱────◦────⊰

Store your shoes in the boxes they came in. It makes it easy to identify them, and they stay clean.

And yet a little tumult, now and then, is an agreeable quickener of sensation; such as a revolution, a battle, or an adventure of any lively description.

Lord Byron (1788–1824)

Corn starch is one of those magical ingredients that's inexpensive and useful for all kinds of things other than thickening gravy. Buy a jar for your bathroom, where it will serve you well in place of talc, as well as for your kitchen.

Take a look at what's hanging in your closet and think about how it might best be accommodated. Install poles at different levels, use the door for hanging a shoe bag (which you might use for many things other than shoes), and add shelves and cubbies.

Little boys rarely need a hanging rod in their closet. One blazer doesn't merit the amount of space a rod consumes. Instead, hang the few dress-up items in your own closet and fill your child's closet with lots of shelves and cubbies. Shallow shelves make everything much more accessible than drawers. And wherever possible, hang pegs . . . for bathrobes, jackets, shirts, pants, and anything else with a loop on it.

Keep everyone's linen on a shelf in the closet of the room in which it's used. You'll never have to go rummaging through a crowded linen closet.

⊱—◦—◦—⊰

Move a chest of drawers into your closet. It frees up space in the bedroom and makes use of all that empty area under the high hanging rods.

⊱—◦—◦—⊰

Keep a file for each pet. It's the place to store all their medical files, including records of vaccinations, weight, birth history, and so on.

Housecleaning

Think about housecleaning tasks in terms of four categories: what needs to be done every day, what needs to be done every week, what needs to be done every month, and what needs to be done once or twice a year.

⊱—◦—◦—⊰

When you must do an unpleasant task, try to team it up with something pleasurable. Listen to good music while you clean the the bathroom. Watch your favorite TV show while you fold laundry. Talk on the phone while you're ironing.

⊱—◦—◦—⊰

List every weekly cleaning chore on a piece of paper and make copies. Each week, have every family member choose five or six tasks. Take turns choosing, and be sure to include tasks that younger family members can handle, such as emptying wastebaskets.

If you have chores to do in one area of your home, plan out a route so that you don't end up retracing steps. This takes a few minutes of preparation but saves lots of time.

Organize your cleaning supplies in a basket, including: an all-purpose cleanser, a sponge, a bottle of ammonia, some clean cloths, a bottle of spray cleaner, a floor cleaner, a spray bottle of window cleaner, a razor blade in a holder, a toothbrush, and a pair of rubber gloves. Keep small cleaning baskets in different areas of the house. Each bathroom should have its own sponge, cleanser, toilet bowl brush, and so on.

If penicillin is the original wonder drug, baking soda is its "cleansing" counterpart. There are endless uses for this extremely inexpensive powder. It absorbs refrigerator odors if you keep an open box somewhere on a back shelf, it's useful for all kinds of cleaning tasks (you'll see tips recommending its use elsewhere in this book), and it's absolutely essential for keeping those fluffy cakes fluffy. Next time you go shopping, buy two boxes . . . or more.

Put an old sock on your hand. It makes a great dusting glove for cleaning venetian blinds. In fact, it's good for dusting just about anything. It also makes a great shoe polisher.

Do your most loathsome chores first. You won't have to think about them all day long.

If you have silver flatware, candlesticks, or decorations, buy a silver polishing cloth. These magical cloths require absolutely no messy polish or water. Just rub and enjoy the shine.

Cut back on the chemicals and poisons that you routinely use around your home. Substitute natural and less expensive alternatives. Among these are:

- Drain cleaner — Baking soda or salt followed by boiling water.

- Air freshener — Set vinegar out in an open dish.

- Window cleaner — White vinegar and water or ammonia and water. Wipe with newspapers.

- Oven cleaner — Baking soda, salt, and water.

- Spot remover — Old-fashioned laundry soap takes out spots on clothing. Dishwashing detergent removes spots on rugs.

> *Simplicity of life, even the barest, is not a misery, but the very foundation of refinement; a sanded floor and whitewashed walls and the green trees, and flowery meads, and living waters outside; or a grimy palace amid the same with a regiment of housemaids always working to smear the dirt together so that it may be unnoticed; which, think you, is the most refined, the most fit for a gentleman of those two dwellings?*
>
> **William Morris (1834–1896)**

If you live in a two-story house, keep a vacuum on each level. It saves huge amounts of time and energy.

━━◦━━

Old toothbrushes are especially useful for cleaning the grout between tiles in the bathroom and on kitchen counters, and that gross stuff from around the base of the faucets.

━━◦━━

There's something spectacular about really clean windows. The problem is that it's a daunting job. The following hints make it considerably simpler ... which makes the pleasure of sitting in your living room on a sunny day and looking out the window much more within your reach!

- Always wash and dry one side of the window vertically and the other side horizontally. It's easier to identify where the streaks are.

- Wait for the sun to go down to wash your windows. The sun will cause streaking.

- Although some people don't agree, I'm a great fan of using newspaper for window washing and wiping. Something in the newsprint really makes them shine.

- Always work from the top down. It helps avoid drips.

Laundry

If your children have laundry baskets in their rooms, they can keep track of (and even *do*) their own laundry. It also eliminates clutter on the floor.

Buy your child white socks only. This will save you the time of searching for mates when you take them out of the dryer. If you have more than one child, buy permanent laundry markers and assign each child a color. Make a large red dot on the toes of one child's socks, a large black dot on the toes of another child's, and so on until it's easy to separate them all.

If you use cloth napkins, get a different napkin ring for each member of the family and have them return their napkins to the ring after breakfast and lunch. By the end of dinner, they will probably be ready for the laundry.

Whenever possible, dry your laundry outside in the sun. All those clichés about sweet-smelling laundry are true; but more important, the energy savings are significant. You'll be shocked by how efficient the sun is.

If you're ever in the position of designing or remodeling a house, put the laundry somewhere upstairs near the bedrooms. Think about where most of your laundry is generated. Whoever developed the notion that the laundry should be in the basement clearly had a maid!

If you do lots of laundry, you may have an impulse to cram as much as you can into the washer and dryer. In fact, doing that is considerably less efficient. Leave enough room for the clothing to toss. It will wash cleaner and dry faster.

A sleeping bag is a great alternative to linen for a child's bed. There's no issue about "making the bed." They can just roll it up and throw it in a closet. And you can wash it every other week and toss it in the dryer.

When stuffed animals are really dirty, gather a few of them together inside a pillowcase, tie a knot on the end, and run them through the washer and dryer that way. They'll come out fluffier than if you washed them without any protection. If the stuffed animals are clean but dusty, just run them through the dryer on the fluff cycle with a sheet of fabric softener inside the pillowcase.

If you're buying a new dryer, keep in mind that even though electric dryers are cheaper at the outset, gas dryers are considerably less expensive to operate.

Home Maintenance and Repair

Do your own wallpapering. If you're handy, it isn't very difficult, and it can transform your environment.

If you've ever had a hard time hitting the nail on the head, poke it through the edge of a piece of cardboard. You can hold onto the cardboard while you're hammering and pull the cardboard away once the nail is securely set in the wood.

Painting a room can transform it. Here are some methods for simplifying what can be an unpleasant chore.

• Turn the paint can upside down for twenty-four hours before you begin painting. Mixing will be much easier.

• To remove decals from a wall before you paint, use lukewarm vinegar.

• Make a paste of salt, boiling water, and alum to fill cracks in floors before you paint them. It will set as hard as concrete.

• Glue a paper plate to the bottom of your paint can (you can use some of the paint as glue). It will catch drips and offer a handy resting place for your brush.

• If you're painting the trim around window panes, rub some soap around the edges of the glass. Any paint that splashes onto it will be easily removed with a soft cloth.

• Keep a file card for each room of the house and write down the paint brand and color formula for the walls, ceiling, and woodwork. Do the same with wallpaper — manufacturer, where you bought it, how many rolls it took to paper the room, and how much it cost. This is useful information if you ever need to match up anything.

• If you're painting steps, begin by painting every other step, letting it dry, and then painting the remaining ones. This technique enables everyone to walk by without injuring the paint.

• If you're planning to resume painting within twenty-four hours, wrap your messy brushes in foil or plastic and stick them in the freezer for your next painting session. Just make sure you allow some time for them to thaw out before use.

Before you attempt to remove melted wax from a wood table top, heat it up a bit with a hair dryer. It will come off much more easily.

Keep an electric hair dryer near your wood stove or fireplace. If you set it on low, it makes a great bellows.

One of the worst things about shoveling snow is knocking the snow off the blade of the shovel. You can avoid the problem by coating the shovel blade with floor wax before you start. The snow will slide right off.

If the speakers on your stereo rattle, take off whatever covers the cones and have a look. Chances are there's a tear or tiny crack in the cone that can be easily mended with some clear nail polish.

If you don't use the entire garage for your car, consider setting up a workbench in it. Make sure you've got a heating source, adequate light, and pegboard for hanging tools, shelves, and lots of other things.

Keep a basic tool kit including the following: electric drill/screwdriver; glue gun; hammer; pliers; plunger, crescent, and pipe wrench; screwdrivers; tape measure; small assortment of screws; small assortment of nails.

Silhouette your tools on a pegboard and you'll always know where things go, what you have, and what's missing.

Punch holes in the manuals that come with your fridge, stove, microwave, TV, and so on, and keep them in a ringbinder on a kitchen shelf.

To prevent the back of what you're drilling through from splintering, put a scrap of any kind of wood (composite board, plywood, etc.) behind it.

If you still can get your hands on the sleeves from old LPs (remember those?), use them to store extra circular saw blades.

If there's a tiny hole in your screen, try dabbing it with some clear nail polish.

The best way to store small quantities of nails, screws, nuts, and bolts is to save small jars and screw the jar lids onto the bottom of a shelf above your workbench. Fill the jars with the objects and screw them onto their lids.

Either buy or make reels for your garden hoses, electric extension cords, and Christmas lights. There is nothing more frustrating than trying to untangle one of these snakes when you're pressed for time.

When you work with an electric saw or grinding wheel (regardless of whether it's a table-top or a hand-held model), stand to the side while you're cutting rather than in front. Saws and grinders can throw a piece of wood or stone in the path of their rotation.

Dip the wooden handles of your favorite garden tools into a pail of bright-colored paint. Red or orange are great. You'll never have trouble finding your tools wherever you may have dropped them.

It pays to have really good garden tools, even if they're a bit more expensive at the outset. Once you have them, however, you've got to take good care of them. Fill a pail with sand and a quart of motor oil. Whenever you finish a day's gardening, use your tools to mix up the sandy oil. It will protect them from rust and lengthen their life considerably.

You can avoid spending hours untangling your garden hose, and also avoid the cost of an expensive hose winder, by nailing a sturdy five-gallon plastic bucket to the wall of your home or shed. Wrap the hose around the bucket.

If you have a cat or dog that likes to roll in your delphiniums, stand a circle of sticks around the base of the plant. It looks pretty and keeps the beasts away.

⊢⊷⊶O⊷⊶⊣

Line your cat's litter box with a garbage bag and fasten it around the rim with an elastic band. When it's time to empty the box, just remove the elastic, lift, and twist.

Safety

Carry a recent photo of your child in your car or wallet. No one plans for a child to get lost, but it's best to be prepared.

⊢⊷⊶O⊷⊶⊣

If you're at a public place such as an amusement park or an historic site or battlefield, your older children may want to be independent. Make sure they have a buddy, and have them wear a bright-colored shirt so that you can spot them from far away.

⊢⊷⊶O⊷⊶⊣

Sit down with your family and talk about what to do if there's a fire. Escape plans can truly save lives. Make sure that all children's rooms have stickers identifying them as such on the windows; and wherever possible, have escape ladders installed that you know how to use.

⊢⊷⊶O⊷⊶⊣

If you ride a bicycle, carry your name, address, and phone number in a seat pack — and wear a helmet! In case of a fall and loss of consciousness, witnesses can help.

Keep a list of emergency numbers taped onto the receiver of each phone in your home. Make it a point to instruct your children on what these numbers are and how and when to use them.

Research by the National Crime Prevention Institute indicates that most burglars will not work longer than sixty seconds trying to break into a home. This is a good case for good locks. Make sure to:

- Lock the door when you leave your home.
- Use high-quality padlocks on garages, sheds, and gates.
- Buy security bars for sliding patio doors.
- Buy deadbolt locks that feature interlocking chassis and full one-inch throws.
- Remember, it isn't worth economizing on locks. If you get good and sick of spending money on security devices, it may be time to move. There are still places you can live where people don't bother to lock their houses.

Be prepared for a power outage due to a storm. Make certain you can get your hands on a flashlight, candles, matches, water, and adequate food. Many supermarkets sell boxed milk, which is great to have on hand for an emergency.

It's a good idea for each member of your family to have a flashlight in her/his bedroom. Check the batteries when you replace the ones in your smoke detectors.

Keep a pillow, blanket, and extra pair of socks and gloves in the trunk of your car. Even if you're not in an accident, you may be able to help someone who is.

<hr/>

Learn the Heimlich maneuver to aid a choking victim. You'll feel more confident in general.

<hr/>

Learn your blood type and make a note of it on your driver's license. If you're ever in a car accident and unable to speak, it's something the police at the scene will be likely to notice.

<hr/>

Write down the numbers of all of your credit cards and put them in a safe place. Better yet, photocopy the cards onto a single sheet and file it.

<hr/>

Kids like to play in driveways. They're the perfect place for chalk drawings and pick-up basketball games. Make it a habit to put a trash can at the foot of the driveway whenever you transform it into a playground. That way you won't have to worry about careless surprise guests or anyone who's using your driveway as a turn-around.

Cars

Try not to wash or polish your car in the sun. The wax and soap will cake, and regardless of how much effort you put into it, you won't end up with a sparkling finish.

Choose some or all of the following items to keep in your car:

- A nylon zippered bag filled with a roll of paper towels and window cleaner.

- A large trash bag (aside from filling it with garbage, you can always cut a hole in the top and two holes in the side to wear as a poncho in the event of a surprise thunderclap).

- A new toothbrush and some dental floss in the glove compartment (if someone is headed to a sleepover but forgot a toothbrush, or if you're going to a meeting/party and want to have a fresh feeling in your mouth, you'll have what you need).

- An extra pair of hosiery.

- A packet of wet towelettes.

- A list of videos you might rent someday.

- A few dollars for just-in-case.

- An empty coffee can with a candle and matches in the trunk (in the event of an emergency, it's a great little furnace).

- An inexpensive disposable camera (if you're ever in an accident, you'll be able to photograph the accident scene; or it might come in handy if you spot a moose by the side of the road).

- If you have small children, a change of clothing for each (you never know when a foot will get soaked in a puddle).

- A note pad for jotting down things you'll need to do at work the next day (once you get home, you can really close the office door).

- Road maps in a zippered envelope.

If your dog drools all over the car, help him overcome the anxiety by just getting in the car and having a cozy time, without actually driving anywhere.

When you clean your car, use baking soda to polish the chrome. It's very effective and enormously satisfying.

If your car has a cruise control switch, be sure to use it whenever you're on a highway. It will help you avoid speeding tickets as well as insure that you're driving in the most economical way possible . . . without lots of variation in speed.

It's always a good idea to get a little bottle of touch-up paint from your car dealer for nicks and scratches. If you can't get the paint, however, go through a giant box of Crayolas and pick a color that's close. Work it into the scratch to prevent rust.

If you live in an area with snowy winters, keep a bag of kitty litter in the trunk just in case you need some extra traction.

> *An ounce of action is worth a ton of theory.*
>
> **Friedrich Engels (1820–1895)**

Family Living

Teach your children how to prepare a basic meal (peanut butter on bread, or pasta with heated-up sauce from a jar) and how to do the laundry before they reach the age of ten. They can do it . . . and they should.

If your kids are ready to head off for school with a bright red juice mustache decorating their upper lip, try getting it off with a washcloth and a small amount of toothpaste. The toothpaste tastes much better than soap, and it's a very effective cleanser for all kinds of food stains including tomato juice and ice pops.

If you have two children who share a closet, paint each half of the rod a different color to prevent fights.

Whatever time your children wake up, make sure you wake up about a half-hour earlier. Those early peaceful moments energize you for the day ahead. (A note to parents of adolescents: If your children wake up between noon and 2 PM, this obviously doesn't apply to you!)

If you have teenagers, put a timer in the bathroom to remind them that it isn't their exclusive throne room — and that showers shouldn't last too long.

Keep a file on each of your children. That's the place to to put report cards, special drawings, newspaper clippings, and any other of the very select things you decide to save.

Keep a folder for all important school information — especially those papers that contain phone numbers or statements about school policy that might come into question over the course of the year, and notices of school events. Keep the folder near the table or desk where your child unloads his/her backpack each day, and go through it at least once a week to keep it current.

Keep the center tube from a roll of paper towels in your car. It's great for transporting a child's artwork home from school undamaged.

A painless way to remove an adhesive bandage is to saturate it with a cotton ball dipped in either baby oil or vegetable oil. It's truly ouchless.

Schedule a regular family meeting every Sunday evening after dinner. Make this the time you go over the calendar for the coming week and figure out who has to be where and how they're getting there. This is also a good time to talk about problems: sibling fights, schedule pressures, and so on. Remember, the purpose of these meetings is to work things out productively . . . not to complain or accuse.

The research is consistent: children who have parents available to help with homework when they need it are better students in the long run. Don't get over-involved and actually do the work for your children, but let them know that when it comes to homework, you're an available resource.

⊱──⊱◈⊰──⊰

Keep a large, erasable calendar on the kitchen wall and assign each member of the family a different-color erasable marker. The colors make it easy to see exactly who has to be where, when.

⊱──⊱◈⊰──⊰

Establish a regular time for homework. It can be one-half hour after your child returns from school, right after dinner, or any other time that your child feels is best. The key is to be consistent. This kind of work habit pays off throughout the school years.

⊱──⊱◈⊰──⊰

Even young children can learn how to file things, and it's a lesson that will serve them well as they get older. File baskets can be bought that sit on desks; beginning with kindergarten, you can teach your children to file drawings, ideas for stories, and anything else that interests them. As they get older, the file can be divided up by subject: To Do, Tests, and Completed Work. (Keep in mind that kids who know how to file can help file family papers as well!)

⊱──⊱◈⊰──⊰

Delegate responsibilities, even though there may be lots of things that no one can do as well as you. The question is, does it really matter that things are done as well as you alone can do them? Always ask for help, and don't be too critical of the kind of job others do. In fact, seize the opportunity to do something entirely frivolous yourself.

> *He who can take no great interest in what is small will take false interest in what is great.*
>
> **John Ruskin (1819–1900)**

Make toy cleanup easy for your children. Begin by establishing a place for everything. If you've got a Lego-maniac, make a Lego-bin. Art supplies can go in a plastic sweater box. Stuffed animals are fine on the bed. Work it out with your child ahead of time, and make sure there isn't so much stuff as to make the task overwhelming.

It's not a good idea to keep toys in a toy box. They're too deep to be useful for finding things. Instead, put up simple wooden shelves. The toys on them make a great-looking decor, and it's easy for kids to find what they're looking for. Toys with small pieces can be stored in duffle-type bags or toolboxes.

If you go to a public event such as a concert or baseball game with your children, pin their ticket stubs onto their jackets. If they get lost, someone can help them back to their seat.

If you've got a teenager who doesn't always check in, it might be worthwhile to invest in a beeper. The understanding is, of course, that when you beep, he or she goes immediately to the nearest phone to report in. It's not cheap, but peace of mind often comes with a price.

Travel

If you travel frequently, make a master list of everything and anything you might ever take with you, including such things as: makeup, moisturizer, shampoo, alarm clock, money belt. Before you begin to pack, check off the things you'll need on this particular journey.

><

Never pack valuables or essential medications in luggage that you check. Always keep it on your person. If your luggage gets lost, you won't have to search for a drug store or worry about your grandmother's diamond engagement ring.

><

If you have the same luggage as most of the other people on your flight, think about how you can distinguish it on the baggage carousel. Balloons obviously won't work, but a big red web belt strapped around the bag might save time and confusion.

><

As you pack your suitcase, make certain to keep a running list of everything that goes in. Keep one copy at home and another in your wallet. If your luggage gets lost, you'll have a good accounting of what was in it. And you'll have a checklist to help you keep track of everything.

><

The time to check the zippers and handles on your luggage is a few weeks *before* you head off on your trip. There's nothing more frustrating than attempting to make your way across a foreign airport with a handleless suitcase.

Always make an effort to get a fix on the identity of your cab driver. In some cities there is an identifying number clearly visible in the back of the cab. In others the driver's number and name are posted in front. However you do it, try to identify the person who's driving you around. If you leave something in the cab, your effort will be rewarded. You'll save yourself hours of searching and a lot of grief.

———○———

If you travel out of the country with any frequency, you'll probably find it useful to own:

- An electrical converter for high-wattage appliances (hair dryers, irons, coffee heaters, etc.) and another one for low-wattage appliances (radios, shavers, contact lens sterilizers, etc). These should cost between $15 and $20 each.

- A worldwide adapter plug kit, which includes a set of five plugs to adapt to wall outlets virtually anywhere in the world.

- An adjustable money belt with pockets for cash, traveler's checks, passport, and credit cards.

- A money exchange calculator, which shouldn't cost more than $20.

- A travel alarm clock.

———○———

Bring along an extra pair of eyeglasses when you go on a trip. Short of that, make certain you have your lens prescription with you.

Before you go on a trip, check with your doctor about any prescriptions you might bring along. If, for example, you're traveling with a child who is prone to ear infections, bring along the Rx for amoxicillin . . . or better yet, fill the Rx before you leave and bring along the medication. Better to have it and not use it than need it and not have it.

Keep your passport in a very safe place while you're abroad. There's an incredible black market for U.S. passports, and the streets of foreign cities are filled with people dedicated to keeping that market strong.

Find out where you can get $25 of the currency for wherever you're going, and get it before you take off.

Keep a large cosmetic case, already packed with everything you need. It's ready to go: toothpaste and brush, shampoo, nonprescription medication, adhesive bandages, sewing kit, antiseptic ointment, tampons, shower cap, deodorant, moisturizer, and whatever else you regard as essential.

Hotel/motel security is an increasing problem. Try hanging the "Do Not Disturb" sign on the doorknob if you leave your room in the evening. Chances are you won't have any unwelcome visitors.

P_{ack} a nightlight. Finding your way around a strange, pitch-black room in the middle of the night can lead to injury.

⊳⋅⬦⋅○⋅⬦⋅⊲

I_f you're traveling by air on a shoestring, leave some room in your schedule so that you can volunteer to be bumped. Airlines usually overbook. When you arrive at the gate, go to the attendant on duty and let him/her know that if they've overbooked you'd be willing to wait for the next flight. Don't wait for a request, but volunteer early. If you get selected, you're likely to get a free flight as a thank-you. And if you and your entire family are selected, you can all get airfare for a free vacation at a future date!

⊳⋅⬦⋅○⋅⬦⋅⊲

P_{ack} several self-closing plastic bags of various sizes. They come in handy for wet bathing suits, wash clothes for sticky hands, leaky bottles, and many, many more things.

⊳⋅⬦⋅○⋅⬦⋅⊲

F_{or} short trips, pack only clothes that go together. If your clothing is either black and white, for example, you'll only need black shoes and will have room for different accessories to change the look.

Index